The Financial Guide to Working Overseas

How to legally avoid tax, invest wisely, build your career, and work abroad successfully

By Rick Todd

Commonsensical Publishing, Los Angeles, California, USA

www.expatinvesting.org

This book is for informational and entertainment purposes only. The author is not an investment advisor or a financial advisor. For financial or legal advice for your specific situation, seek a relevant professional.

Table of Contents

OVERVIEW

In today's decaying economy everyone at one time or another has considered moving abroad to improve their income and expand their career. Others still view working abroad as a chance to explore a new culture and to have exciting adventures they can tell their friends and family in years to come. Others are simply sick and tired of the same boring existence and see living abroad as a change of pace and the possibility to **reinvent oneself**.

Working abroad is all these things. For many, it is the most exciting thing you will do in your life. You will interact with new cultures, eat new and exciting cuisines, and possibly improve your standard of living dramatically. Your income may go up, you may be able to afford a servant for the first time, and if you are single you may be able to meet a partner and lover unlike any you could have met back home.

The Financial Guide to Retiring Abroad

Working abroad can also be **hell on earth**. The weather might be depressingly cold, or brutally hot. You may be used to living in a more open and liberal society, and are now confronted with a closed and conservative one. You may be overwhelmed by the pollution and poverty of your new home. And finally, your job may surround you with incompetents and foreigners who neither understand you nor know how to work professionally.

So is it worth it? Only time will tell. I lived abroad for four years across three different countries and three widely different cultures. I'm American and to me living in London, Dubai and Bahrain was a mix of excitement, boredom, happiness and misery unlike anything I'd ever experienced. **The journey changed me forever**. I didn't do that many touristy things like ride camels through pyramids or visit strange holy temples. I worked with the local people in an office. I drove to work. I put my money in a bank. I lived what most would describe as a very normal lifestyle. Only I did it 12 time zones away from the place where I was born and raised.

The idea for this book came about from my first book **The Financial Guide to Retiring Abroad**. I realized that there are many people who are working abroad, and have a need for good personal financial advice to help them get ahead. I've taken the material from The Financial Guide to Retiring Abroad that concerns investment and tweaked it for someone who is in the midst or beginning of their career. I've also added my experience in working for several years in Europe and the Middle East, and taken the knowledge of the hundreds of expats I came to know in my travels.

I've also added a section on working in a war zone, a lucrative but **dangerous** career path for hundreds of thousands of people. The wars in Afghanistan and Iraq have led to an entire industry of contract workers who earn far more than their counterparts back in safe countries, but who encounter danger and death almost every day in their work overseas.

Who is this book for?

This book is really for anyone who is looking to move overseas and work. In the following pages I will look at the various aspects of life overseas for the expatriate. An expatriate or **expat** is a person who has moved away indefinitely from his or her home country. I'm going to use the term throughout this book to describe you. An expat is a nice way of saying **immigrant** but it is also more commonly used for westerners who have moved abroad for their careers. Immigrant is a dirty word usually used to describe someone from the developing world who moved to a richer country to make ends meet. In reality there's not that much difference between an expat and an immigrant, particularly in the eyes of the law in many countries, so don't fool yourself.

This book is not for retirees or people who wish to live for only part of the year abroad. It is also not for those who wish to purchase a vacation property abroad. **This book is for people who wish to have a career abroad.** Working abroad is an immense undertaking. It may require you to learn a **foreign language**. It may mean changing the way you dress, acclimatizing yourself to markedly different weather and food, and even changing your sleep patterns. It is not for everyone, and it is certainly not for those who are **timid** or **ignorant.**

Westerners

This book however is primarily for westerners. Why? Well, I'm a westerner and my experience overseas can only really be helpful to other westerners. We have different visa requirements for travel, the jobs open to us are usually higher paying, and we have bigger egos. Maybe there are a lot of differences after all between expats and immigrants on second thought.

I define a westerner as a person who has spent most of his or her life in a developed country. Westerner is no longer a racial classification as the countries that make up the West are diverse, and in some cases, no longer even located in the west. Also, westerners are always citizens of these countries. This is an important point, as having a **western passport** is a very important tool that will help you successfully settle in another country in retirement. Sadly, the world is divided into a giant class system, and those with passports from the developed world are given a great deal of access to developing countries, while those with only developing world passports are given highly restricted (if any) access at all to the developed world.

As a westerner, your passport is a source of immense power and prestige. It can be a legal defense that gives you far more rights than the average citizen of the country you wish to move to. But it can also make you a target for crime and considerable scrutiny. When you travel and retire to a poorer part of the world as a westerner you will be seen as someone with **more wealth** than most (even if that is not really the case), and you will be seen as someone who is **more professional and better educated** than most (again, even if that is not the case). Behave accordingly.

The other reason this book is for westerners is that western economies are very different than developing ones. This book is written primarily as a **financial guide** for an expat. There are quite a few travel guides out there that tell you the best places to go in terms of weather, food and nightlife, but there aren't many that discuss the financial aspects of living overseas.

Overview

As an expat you have to worry about your pension contributions, your taxes and your investments.

In the pages ahead I plan to talk about all these things. I'll also discuss visas and visa requirements for various parts of the world. I'll also give you general, but good advice on **where to put your money** and **where not to put your money**. As an expat you will be tempted by slick salesmen attracted to your high (or relatively high) salary who will want to part you from your hard earned cash. Don't be fooled. Almost always the best place to invest is to **invest back home**. I'll explain why later.

Property

And what about property? Is property a good investment? The answer to that is generally **no.** In almost every expat guidebook you will be told that buying property is a great idea. Sometimes it is, but most of the time it is not. It really depends on your situation and your career. In many countries foreigners are not even allowed to purchase property at all, and you have to take that into consideration. I will go into great detail about this in the next chapter.

Retirement

When you decide to retire, you are going to have to make a decision as to where you want to live. Should you stay abroad or move back home? I'll briefly go into the decisions you'll need to make from a financial standpoint.

*For more in-depth information on the subject, check out my book on retirement: **The Financial Guide to Retiring Abroad**. It's available on Amazon.com and in e-book format through my website, www.expatinvesting.org*

Working abroad is an enormous challenge. Every day tens of thousands of people from around the world move to another country for an indefinite period of time for better opportunities and new adventures. Unfortunately they are faced with an almost total lack of good information on how to get settled and how to manage their money.

Why you were right to buy this book

There isn't a great deal of information on where and how to invest properly, particularly if you are living for an indefinite period overseas. Most of the information that purports to be about investing is written by con artists and charlatans and is exhorting you to buy property. In general you should ignore them.

In the chapters below I'll discuss how to invest properly. Fortunately, the rules on investing apply universally, and are easy to learn. Many of the investments you hear about on the news or see in advertisements such as **off shore accounts, hedge funds, and gold** are not wise investments and should be disregarded. The general rule when it comes to investing is that if you see a bright and flashy advertisement about an investment on a billboard or on television, **it's best to ignore it**. I'll explain why.

Taxes and their crucial importance

Taxes are one of the many reasons people move to work in other countries. In general, developing countries have lower tax rates than developed ones. Taxes should be at the forefront of your decision to move to a country. In this book I will look at the various **tax havens** throughout the world and how moving to them should be a key consideration. If you are an American you are required by law to continue to pay taxes **even if you live abroad**. Also, depending on the state you formerly lived in, you may even owe state income tax. The United States is one of the few countries out there that continues to tax its citizens no matter where they live. As bad as this seems, there are still considerable tax benefits for an American living abroad **as long as he or she chooses to live in a country that is tax-friendly to foreigners.**

Other westerners can avoid taxes altogether. However, this only kicks in if they live in their new country for a certain period of time, and over the course of most of the year. These are things rarely mentioned in travel guides, and if they are, they are only glossed over.

This is not a book about becoming rich

Sorry, but I don't know the secret to becoming rich, and I really don't know how to get rich by living abroad. But if I did know the secret, do you think I would tell you for the nominal price of a book? Probably not.

This is a book about how to keep what you've earned, and to prepare for a well funded retirement. In my time abroad I never heard of an expat who got rich buying property as an investment. I also never heard of an expat who moved abroad and found a job that made him a millionaire. I have met highly paid expats in big and important jobs. I'd say they were well compensated, but hardly wealthy.

The truth is that as an expat you will increase your income by a significant percentage, but you may also give up many of the advantages of staying in your home country. When you move abroad you won't understand how to invest your money, you may need to sign up for your new country's pension system, and you'll more than likely be an employee rather than a self-employed businessperson. The odds are stacked against the possibility that you'll strike it rich.

You'll also be faced with **temptations** to spend more. Many people who move abroad for better jobs find that much of the new income they realized is being spent on frivolous things like a bigger home, more parties, and a fancier car. Many expats find that their new life is simply a means of living a more exciting life, rather than helping their bottom line.

This book will endeavor to give you the advice you need to stay on track and not fritter away a period in your life where you can make more money and prepare for a better future. I'm not trying to come off as a downer who will tell you to not spend your money. Far from it. Some of the best times I had abroad were due to the fact that I was spending money on myself from a higher than normal salary. This book is simply going to make sure that if you decide to save some of your income, you will know the best places to put it, and how to avoid the worst places.

Definitions

Throughout this book I will use the terms "developed", "developing", "third world", and "first world". These are important terms and it is essential that you know their definitions. Forgive me if you already do, and simply skip this section.

The terms "first world" and "developed" are interchangeable, with the former term being considered old fashioned and the latter term more modern. They refer to the parts of the world where people live well and have easy access to modern technology. This part of the world includes the United States and Canada, Australia and New Zealand, Western Europe and the nations within it, Japan, Singapore, Hong Kong, and by some definitions South Korea, Taiwan, and Israel. You might also include the parts of the world that are either closely associated with, or entirely governed by the United States or Western European powers such as France and the United Kingdom. Examples of these would be Barbados, the Cayman Islands, the Virgin Islands (both British and American), New Caledonia, Tahiti, etc. These areas are almost always islands, and often times run their economies on a mixture of tourism and offshore financial services. More on these later.

As you might have guessed, the remainder of the world is "developing" or the "third world." Just because a country is not in the developed world does not mean that it is poor. On the contrary: the country with the highest per capita income in the world is Qatar, in the Persian Gulf. However, no one would consider that nation to be developed. Being developed does not only mean being relatively wealthy. It also means having **transparent laws**, a democratic system of government, a diverse economy, and a fair legal system. The vast majority of countries that are seen as developing are either poor, unfair to many of the people who reside within their borders, or both.

Many of the recommendations I make in this book will refer to the developing world, rather than the developed world. The differences between the developing world and the developed world are so great, that an **extensive discussion** needs to occur in order for you to be prepared for the transition. If a recommendation I make is valid in any country, including the developed world, I'll make note of it.

Is moving abroad safe?
This is such a broad question that it's too difficult to answer simply and easily. In general moving abroad is fraught with **risk** and, depending on

the country, it can be very dangerous. Many expats choose to move to **war zones** for the lure of high pay.

Most expats will move to another developed country. There's not too great a danger in that. Most developed countries have low levels of street crime (the United States is an exception but its crime is located primarily in impoverished urban areas and is easy to avoid), and the most danger you'll probably face is having to drive on a different side of the road, than you're used to.

Moving to the developing world can be another issue entirely. You'll have to deal with a workplace environment very different from your own. You'll have to deal with traffic that is extremely dangerous and virtually lawless. You'll have to live in an environment that is probably polluted, corrupt and incompetent.

No guide can prepare you for your new country completely. What I can offer is my own background in working abroad, an overview of the financial aspects of life as an expat, and a dollop of common sense to go with it all. The rest is up to you.

The economics of moving abroad

Personal finance for an expat has several important differences from personal finance for someone who doesn't move overseas. For one, there is the issue of dealing with a foreign bank. For another, there is the issue of healthcare, which is often more expensive and private rather than public. And then there is the issue of your state pension. If you live abroad, you will not necessarily be able to make contributions to it through taxes. Living abroad makes investing for retirement a **vital issue**.

Overview

If you are not disciplined enough to save money in your years abroad, you might very well be broke when you reach retirement.

In our new age of fiscal responsibility, governments all over the world are restricting individuals' access to **offshore** bank accounts and demanding that their citizens report all income and savings to the relevant tax authorities. Many governments (particularly the United States) view their citizens living abroad as potential **tax evaders** or even potential **terrorists**. This book is not an instruction manual on how to evade taxes. It is rather a basic guide on how to legally avoid tax whenever possible. And throughout, I will remind you to let your government know the location of all your assets so that you are obeying the law and paying what your government considers its fair share.

Politics

A word about politics. For some expats moving abroad is a political statement. Those who believe in free and unfettered capitalism will move abroad to avoid tax. Others will see moving abroad as going to live in a new and more sophisticated culture. Both groups have their beliefs and their wants and needs. I personally can sympathize with both groups. However, this book is not a political tract. It is an effort to give you the best information available on living overseas as an expat, from a financial point of view. It is this information that is more important than any other when it comes to living and prospering overseas.

Should you move overseas?

Moving overseas is not for everyone. Not everyone can handle the change of pace, the myriad new customs, and if moving to a developing country from a wealthier nation, the intense poverty that besets most of the world.

The Financial Guide to Retiring Abroad

Most expats, male and female, are **single and young**. That is not to say middle-aged expats with families are not in abundance: they are certainly found everywhere. It is simply common sense that it is easier for someone with no family ties and little in the way of debt or property holding back to move quickly to anywhere in the world at a moment's notice.

I would not become an expat if I had any of the following:

1. **A severe medical condition or handicap.** That includes mental illnesses/handicaps. Moving abroad will mean dealing with a completely different culture, not just on the street but also within the medical establishment. Treatment varies from country to country, and that includes developed country to developed country. As an American who used the UK's NHS I expected to have easy access to medicine like that I had in the US. I was wrong. UK doctors do not see medicine as a replacement for treatment the way American doctors tend to. My medical condition was a minor one, and the NHS's stinginess was at first annoying, but I grew to accept their way of thinking and determined that my American doctor was too quick to see prescription drugs as a solution to any illness. You may disagree, and find changing to different healthcare systems too jarring.

2. **A loved one who is gravely ill**. If one of your parents were to die while you live abroad, the effect might be devastating. You might blame yourself, probably unreasonably, in some way for the death. Reconsider moving abroad until your loved one's condition is no longer an issue.

3. **You have problems with the law.** If you have a criminal background, you will probably not be granted a work permit,

particularly in the developed world. In our post 9/11 environment background checks that make use of INTERPOL data are commonplace. It is quite common for a work permit, permanent residency or any other type of visa to be rejected on the basis of the criminal background of the applicant.

4. **A lack of an education.** While different countries have different opportunities for individuals based on their education, and in a foreign country the university you attended may not be as well known as it is in your home country, having an education is essential to avoiding being given a low paying unskilled labor position. Many people who have never worked abroad will be surprised to learn that in general **the schools you attended are not important.** The exception to that is if you attended the best universities in your country, and by best I mean the top ten highest ranked institutions. Even then, the universities you attended may not be well known outside your country. I doubt the vast majority of Americans can name the best university in Germany. But having the degree is what will count at the end of the day, and not having it will hurt your job prospects.

5. **A lack of work experience**. Experience is essential to being a successful expat. Expats are generally in the middle of their careers, particularly if they are from Western countries. Expats at the beginning of their careers are not wanted because a company views the hiring of an expat as the means to bring on immediately workable talent. You can also have **too much** experience by being an expat in the latter part of your career. At this point age discrimination will kick in, and countries may view you as too much of a potential burden on their healthcare systems to easily grant a work permit or other visa type.

Are there more opportunities overseas?

In this era of global economic turmoil many people around the world are considering taking jobs overseas in an effort to avoid their own market downturns. But this recession is more severe than most, and is commonly characterized as global in reach. Does that mean that every country has been affected?

I believe that to some extent, yes, every country has been affected, even those that are still reporting tremendous economic growth. If you are thinking of moving overseas to find work, you are most likely not alone, and there will be others with the same idea. The result will be more competition for jobs in any part of the globe. And in most cases a local, native candidate will be chosen over you.

That doesn't mean there's no hope. If you are skilled in your line of work, if you are willing to move to countries that others would find difficult to live in, and if you are willing to make compromises with prospective employers, **you can find work**. But it will be tough. This book can only do so much to get you a job. In the end you will have to find it yourself.

One piece of advice I will give is this: **quantity over quality**. I think that the search for a job is a game. The more places you hit, the more likely you are to find work. The more countries you are willing to work in, the more opportunities. Act accordingly.

This is a guide for financial planning

The primary purpose of this book is to act as a financial planning guide. For too long expats have been at the mercy of bad financial planners who offer investments that are too risky, or laden with ridiculously high fees.

Overview

Financial planning doesn't need to be complex and it usually doesn't require you to hire expensive professional help. There is an additional layer of difficulty in the fact that an expat may be moving frequently or holding his money in a different country to the one he is working in, but the rules are generally the same.

As simple as the rules are, and I'll explain them in upcoming chapters, most expats are relatively clueless as to where to invest their savings. They make silly mistakes such as buying real estate in volatile markets, they make use of local banks, financial exchanges, and other gimmicks. And they put their money in offshore accounts, an often illegal act.

So is moving abroad for work the solution to all your problems?

Working overseas is a life changing event for anyone who does it. It is logical to assume that the more countries you are willing to work in, the more job opportunities there are. But there are prices to pay for working overseas. For one, if and when you decide to move back home again to continue your career, your overseas experience may be **discriminated** against.

What do I mean by that? Many employers, sometimes rightfully sometimes wrongfully, see a prospective employee who has worked abroad as someone who may lack the specialized **native** experience necessary for a job. The common stereotype is that working in a foreign country teaches you a foreign way of doing things. Foreign things are seen as different, inferior, and possibly unprofessional.

The Financial Guide to Retiring Abroad

How do you overcome this stereotype? You can apply to work at companies and organizations that are more internationally focused. If the sector you work in looks at overseas experience as a positive or a necessary part of a career you won't have a problem. But most people who work overseas for significant portions of their career will face the same discrimination an immigrant will face when they return home. You may very well be permanently **tainted** by your overseas experience.

My advice to people who are thinking of working overseas is to look at the experience as a temporary one, or a permanent one. Don't view overseas work in the same way as you would view work in your home country. It is different and everyone will see it as such. Take that into account when you are measuring the impact working overseas will have on your career.

Of course there are many benefits to working overseas. You may very well learn a new way of doing things that will improve your skill set. If you find work in a developing country, you may rise through the ranks faster and gain more managerial experience. You may gain a better picture of the way the global economy works, and can help companies you work for overcome cultural and market differences that hinder trade and commerce. You will almost certainly become a more sophisticated and professional individual.

In the following chapters I will lay out for you the financial basics to surviving and flourishing overseas. The rest is up to you. The advice I am giving you comes from living on three different continents in four different countries. Some of the advice is just good common sense. Most of the advice comes from trial and error that only be gained through a period of living abroad.

Overview

I wish I had had access to this book and its cousin **The Financial Guide to Retiring Abroad** when I lived overseas. I have seen so many expats fritter away their savings in bad investments, overspending, and poor life choices. You don't have to suffer the way I did. Investing is relatively easy once you know the basics. Living abroad makes it a little trickier, but if you apply the rules I lay out in the chapters ahead, you'll do fine.

In the next chapter I'm going to discuss one of the biggest investment issues that face expats working overseas: whether to purchase a property. The world has witnessed a catastrophic fall in real estate prices in country after country in this global economic quagmire. Is it wise to look at property as an investment that can make you healthy profits? **In short, no.** I'll explain why in the next chapter.

The Financial Guide to Retiring Abroad

CHAPTER ONE – REAL ESTATE

Property is **not an investment**. Contrary to what virtually every expat guide, realtor and even many of your fellow expats will tell you, property is not an investment. Rental property is a potential investment. But property that you use for your personal residence should never be viewed as an investment.

What is an investment?

I define an **investment** as equity in an asset you expect to increase in value over time in order to sell at a later date to realize a profit. The property you purchase overseas as your primary residence should be viewed as a roof over your head that you can comfortably afford so that if housing prices drop for any reason, you couldn't care less, as your only concern is maintaining loan payments so you can continue to live in your home.

Inflation hedge

If buying a home is not an investment, what is it? It is an **inflation hedge**. This is a hard concept for many people to grasp as it goes against everything you've been told most of your life. For most people living in the developed world, a home was seen as something that would increase in value over time that you could sell later in life to realize a profit and either buy a bigger home or fund your retirement. The recent almost global housing crash has taught Americans and Europeans that this is a **myth.** Other countries such as Japan have realized this for the past twenty years after seeing housing values decline dramatically to such an extent that they may never return to their previous highs of the 1980s within our lifetime.

Your home should be seen as an inflation hedge, not an investment. When you rent a property, your rent goes up every year. It goes up every year because your landlord wants to make more money, and also because he or she does not wish your rent to be below market rates (what everyone else is paying locally for a similar property). Rents as a whole always go up when an economy is growing because when an economy is growing there is **inflation**. I don't want to get into a long discussion as to why this is, or what the definition of inflation is, but in short, inflation is a natural occurrence that affects everyone through increasing prices of day to day expenses.

If you own a property you don't pay ever-increasing rent. If the property is owned outright, you pay nothing on a regular basis other than maintenance costs. If you have financed the property you will typically be able to lock in a monthly payment that as time goes by, will be lower than renting a comparable residence.

Rent usually stays a constant as a percentage of your income. This is the point of purchasing property: **to reduce the percentage of your income devoted to paying for your housing**. That is the only reason you should ever buy a home to live in.

As an expat you will be tempted by the **dark side** when you live abroad. Expats are naturally drawn to parts of the world experiencing considerable **economic growth**. Increasing real estate values go hand in hand with economic growth, so it makes sense that if you are thinking about buying a property in your new country, you will naturally assume it is a good investment since property prices are skyrocketing.

This is particularly true in the developing world. Property prices in markets that are not highly regulated (as in developing markets) tend to grow very rapidly. But what grows rapidly also **collapses quickly**. The developing world's markets are the most **volatile on earth**. Avoid becoming a victim of them.

I have seen it first hand in my time in Dubai. There many expats viewed the purchase of a property as a good investment. Of course for many it was not to be, and disaster soon followed their purchases.

The story of Dubai

Perhaps one of the greatest examples in recent history of Westerners "investing" in property overseas in order to make a profit and losing their shirts is the example of Dubai. I saw it in my time there. I was fortunate to not be earning enough money to afford a property, which was probably the first red flag to any outside investor. If a local executive earning a decent wage is unable to afford even a basic apartment, the market is probably overvalued.

The second red flag came in the form of **lights.** Dubai sold apartments within **zones** to foreigners. These zones were the only areas where foreigners were permitted to buy property, and even then the properties could only be leased for a 99-year period. Not allowing foreigners to buy property except by lease is a common event in the developing world. It's a draconian way of preventing wealthy foreign companies from buying up cheap land en masse, but it has the nasty **side effect** of preventing small retired or vacation investors from having the same property rights as citizens.

Within these zones giant apartment complexes had been built, but only a few of the rooms ever had their lights on. Why? Most of the apartments had not been purchased by small investors. Instead they had been purchased by **speculators.** Speculators have no interest in buying property to live in. Instead they view property as something to be sold to others in large chunks. When you see giant apartment developments being built within "zones" or in pleasant areas such as beaches or near golf courses or ski slopes, and no lights or other normal activity in them, run away…and fast! You are about to witness a real estate implosion, and it won't be pretty.

No recourse

To make matters worse if you feel you have been duped into buying a property overseas after being fed exaggerations or even lies by a property developer, you will usually have little or no recourse.

Real Estate

Recourse comes in the form of a court settlement, and courts in the developing world are spectacularly slow and corrupt. If you combine that with the **enmity** shown foreign plaintiffs who bought land that is utterly unaffordable to the average person, you can expect little sympathy that you lost your shirt to a local.

Not really an owner

A British friend of mine "purchased" land in Indonesia with several friends in order to build a small resort. The resort had two A-frame huts built on it and was located on an island in one of Indonesia's many archipelagos. In pictures he showed me, it was gorgeous.

The problem was that though he was the caretaker, he was not the owner. Instead of buying the property in some kind of government condoned lease, he and his friends made a deal with a local to purchase the property in the local's name. When shown the money, the local Indonesian readily agreed.

Of course he agreed, because as soon as he got the money, he disappeared. This was not known to my friend who went on and built huts and other elements on the island, **an island he did not even own**. His only recourse was the local Indonesian courts. As of this writing, five years after our initial conversation, he is still without a solution. **Never buy property abroad for investment purposes.**

When you should buy property?

In this era of collapsing housing prices and lackluster performance, many are convinced that buying a home is a terrible idea. In many cases, it is.

However, for some people, buying a home is a (potentially) great idea **so long as your personal situation fits this set of conditions:**

1. **You plan on living in the same place indefinitely.** By that I mean not just the same country but the same town/city. In an era of people changing jobs regularly this might be difficult to impossible. But if you live in a big city, it is doable as there will be more job opportunities available than in a more remote area. And by indefinitely I mean throughout the life of the loan you took to buy the property. In order to see the financial benefit of living in a home you will most likely have to stay in it a decade or more.

2. **You do not plan on moving.** That means staying in the same house for the long run. You don't plan on selling your house for a larger one. Doing so entails usually taking on more debt later in life and closer to retirement. You want to enter retirement debt free if possible as your income will most likely drop somewhat.

3. **You won't borrow against your home.** Even if you have considerable equity in your home and can get great loan terms to borrow against that equity, don't do it.

4. **You do not care if the value of your home plummets.** The point of buying your home was to reduce the part of your budget that you devote to housing. It was not to hope that the value of your home will go up and you will profit. That is **speculation**. For every person who makes money speculating, there are at least three people who lose money. Don't be a speculator.

Most expats will not be able to comply with these conditions. Most expats are "rolling stone" types who gather no moss and are always on the move.

For them, buying property is an anchor of sorts and a purchase of property becomes a liability rather than a benefit.

The key idea behind purchasing property is that you will **save money over time**. When you are in the beginning or middle of your career, you still have time ahead of you to weather market downturns, inflation, and the other financial obstacles expats generally face over the years. Paying off a house loan over time allows you to save substantially over someone renting a comparable property over the same period. However, the key to accomplishing this saving is to **stay in the same property for a considerable period of time**. How long? Generally it takes **10 to 15 years** before you start to see savings compared to someone who is renting.

In some places you simply can't buy

In many countries, foreigners are simply not allowed to buy property. In Mexico, foreigners cannot purchase property near the border or within several kilometers of the beach. In Saudi Arabia, foreigners are not allowed to buy property at all, and in other countries long term leases are the only way to purchase property.

If you live in a country where the only way to "buy" property is in a long term lease, I would never look at it as an investment. The value of the property diminishes dramatically over time if the market knows that the property will revert back to state ownership at some point in the future. Again, if you are confident that you will be living and working in the same area indefinitely, the purchase of property via a long term lease might make sense, **as you are minimizing the part of your budget devoted to housing**. But as an investment to sell to another person at a later date, a lease is a terrible idea.

An example of the affect leasehold zones can have on property prices is **Marina del Rey** in the Los Angeles area. Who would want to buy a property that will revert back to the original owner in only a few years? While this is not a foreign city, is suffers from the same legal issues as any leasehold. Marina del Rey is beachfront property right next to Los Angeles, owned by the county of Los Angeles. The apartments there are quite cheap, yet ideally located. Why are they so cheap? Because when the development was first created, it was placed on a giant leasehold that reverts back to Los Angeles County ownership when it ends. Why pay top dollar for a property that won't be yours in less than a decade or two? And why pay top dollar for a property that no one will be willing to buy from you at all in the future?

Complex legal structures in place of buying property

Another method used to buy property in the developing world is the creation of a complex legal structure that gives a foreigner some of the rights of a citizen in terms of property ownership. As mentioned earlier, in Mexico, foreigners cannot purchase land on the beach or on the border. However, by creating a Mexican corporation, and having two shareholders, a foreigner can then have the corporation purchase property on the foreigner's behalf.

However, even these trusts have time limitations built into them that require renewal. If the government or the people decide that they've had **enough of foreigners** buying their prime land and bidding the prices up, you can bet that a law will be passed forbidding the renewal of the trusts. Another difficulty that might arise would stem from trying to sell this trust-held land. If I was a foreigner deciding to buy land, would I buy land that only had a few years left on a trust? Or would I buy land that allowed me to create a fresh trust with a new, long-term set of time limitations? Probably the latter, and I won't buy it from a foreigner but from a local citizen. The very purchase of a property by a foreigner may drive the value down slightly.

Signs of trouble

Unfortunately, most information on the internet or in books about moving overseas is linked to real estate agents in those countries who are **utterly lacking in scruples or ethics**. They will assure you that the real estate market in their country is safe and secure.

I suggest the following list of red flags that will show you that buying a property in the country you are planning to move to is dangerous:

- No right for foreigners to **actually** own land
- Courts system seen as corrupt and incompetent
- Aggressive sales tactics by local real estate agents
- Large, unfinished apartment blocks with no signs of habitation being built all at once
- Prices rapidly rising and unaffordable for most locals
- No financing available for purchasers
- Real estate agents largely unlicensed

Buying a property is likely the **largest expenditure you will ever make**. Can you afford to sign off on a property in a nonchalant manner simply because all your fellow expats are doing the same thing? Oftentimes renting is the best solution, though even renting a property can be fraught with difficulty.

The issue with renting

We now live in an era where many countries have seen the complete collapse of their housing markets. No new houses are being built, no one is buying what is on the market, and the prices for homes have dropped dramatically. Many people feel that it is best to avoid housing altogether and simply rent for the rest of your life.

Buying a home is a terrible investment, but a great way to save money. Historically housing prices stay relatively constant. It's when the anomaly of housing bubbles come that people become convinced that the purchase of a home is a way to become rich, so long as you can find a buyer at some point in the future. This is the **greater fool theory**. So long as you can find a greater fool than yourself to buy your overvalued property, you'll do okay.

The housing market at this point becomes a giant game of **musical chairs** and when the music stops (a recession starts), whoever is still caught owning a home will be the one in trouble. Many people will have entered this market as investors rather than actual home owners, and will have purchased a home they couldn't afford in order to **flip** it to someone else to make a profit.

Now that the housing market has collapsed, the public is terrified of buying property at all, even though housing prices are probably **undervalued** and a great deal if you buy for the long term. You now see pundits everywhere stating that renting a home is the way to go. The problem with renting is that rent increases will make rent stay a **constant percentage of your budget**. With a property you purchase, you reduce that percentage over time.

Real Estate

Most expats will never own property
Realistically, most expats, particularly those who pick and move from country to country will never own property. Nor should they. Your personal residence should never be viewed as an investment, and because it only benefits you if you own it for a long period of time, many expats will rent for their lifetime.

That's not a bad thing. In many countries renters have considerable rights. In Europe and much of Latin America, as well as parts of Asia, the renter has the right to withhold rent if the home is not taken care of properly by the landlord. In some countries, such as parts of Mexico, if the landlord wishes to sell the property, he must first offer it to the tenant. Many urban areas throughout the world have **rent control** and require rented housing to offer things like heating, clean premises and other elements.

So being a renter is not a bad thing. In many countries, **it is the only option** for expats. Many countries do not allow foreigners to buy land under any conditions, or only allow foreigners to buy property under certain conditions that make the ownership of property more of a burden than a benefit.

Property is an anchor
One of the biggest problems with owning property is that **it makes you stay in one place.** By that I mean that you cannot just pick and up and go if you want to move back home or move to another country. You need to sell your property first. Property has the funny characteristic that when you **really** need to sell it, you're either not able to sell, or you have to sell for less than what you paid.

What makes a person sell property? Usually money troubles. A loss of a job, a loss of income, and you will have to sell. But if your problems are related to an economic downturn, you can bet that everyone around you will be suffering as well. And that means that everyone around you will be selling their property at the same time. When the property market is overloaded with properties for sale, buyers are few and far between.

It would actually be better for you to sell a property for your own personal reasons, rather than economic ones. But even then, if the issue is health-related and you have to return home for treatment, you will not be around to sell your property. You'll be at home hoping someone is successfully selling it for you.

And what about popular unrest? If a country becomes unstable, and you have to leave to avoid getting swept up, you can't take your property with you. Even if the unrest isn't too great, it will certainly scare off potential foreign buyers, and the locals won't have the money to purchase your real estate. When you rent, if you leave unannounced or in a hurry, the only person who loses is your landlord. And there probably isn't a thing he can do to you if you leave the country never to return.

The renting solution

With renting you may feel the property you are living in is not truly yours. But if you think of the lease agreements you would be signing with the government in order to "buy", you would not really be an owner in any form. Remember, at the end of the day in the eyes of a foreign government you are not a citizen but a **guest**. Guests can have their **invitations** revoked at any moment.

Real Estate

Renting from a local landlord gives you one enormous advantage over a foreign property owner/investor: the **ability to leave** at a moment's notice. In my opinion the ability to get out of a foreign country with no delay is the most crucial ability to have when you live and retire abroad. At any given time the country you are living in may:

- Pass laws that restrict foreigners' right to live in the country
- Erupt in revolution
- Suffer an enormous weather disaster that destroys thousands of homes near you and kills tens of thousands more people
- Devalue its currency, wiping out the value of the property

Think it can't happen? As I write this book in 2010, the most popular retirement destination for Americans, Mexico, now is home to the city with the highest murder rate in the world, Ciudad Juarez. Its entire northern border with the United States is largely in the hands of drug lords. Thailand, another popular retirement locale for Westerners, particularly Europeans, is paralyzed by anti-government protests that have resulted in considerable **violence and instability,** with the future of its government in doubt.

Scenes of expats fleeing into their local embassies have been shown on television countless times during our lives. While I am trying not to overstate the dangers of living abroad in order to deter you, I am simply stating that it would be in your best interest to make as little investment in the local economy as possible. You need to be able to flee if you can, and plowing hundreds of thousands of dollars into a property will **cloud your judgment** and make you unable to make to make important decisions when the time comes. Renting takes care of that. The repercussions from breaking an agreement with a local landlord are far less than the repercussions of losing your life's savings.

There is also the benefit of being a **foreigner** and renting. In many countries with a history of socialist governments, there are typically a great many tenant protections. Eviction in these countries is usually exceptionally difficult for a landlord, and tenants take full advantage of these laws. A foreigner, on the other hand, is seen as a temporary and wealthy potential tenant. As a foreigner you may be able to get better deals, and certainly will be responded to by a larger market than a local. You may also have to pay **slightly more** rent than a local if you're not careful, but considering the fact that you have moved abroad to be in a cheaper country, you may still be able to save significant sums of money.

Renting is not without risks. Most people who offer a house to rent may see renting it out as only a temporary situation. They may intend to sell at some point in the future. (An apartment owner will more likely view his property as an income producing asset and will prefer to have long-term tenants. The sale of the property will be far less likely.)

Moving frequently is a huge inconvenience and renting a property leaves open the possibility of being forced to move. But in my opinion there is a substantial difference between **moving** house and **fleeing**. The former you do when your lease ends, the latter you do when you have to abandon a property you own.

If you will only feel comfortable in a house rather than an apartment, I suggest researching who the larger rental property owners are in the area where you wish to move. If they own several homes or villas, they will probably view these properties in the same way they view apartments, and you will less likely be forced to move due to the sale of the house.

What kind of property should I rent?

I think there are three important rules when it comes to determining what type of property you want to rent.

1. Rent an apartment, not a house. Apartments are cheaper, easier to clean, put you closer to your neighbors if you need help, and are more centrally located. A landlord is less likely to sell it from underneath you as well.

2. Pick a unit on the ground floor. As you get older, steps will become a hassle and a safety issue. Ground floor units allow for quick escapes in the event of a fire. Elevator repair is not the best in many parts of the world.

3. Choose an apartment near the places where you shop and more importantly near a quality hospital. Being close to attractions should be less of a concern. You'll probably get bored of them after awhile anyway. Being close to a hospital can save your life.

4. Make an inventory of everything included in the property. If you ever leave and want your security deposit back, you'll have the inventory to prove to the owner that you haven't taken anything. The inventory should also describe the **state** of everything included in the apartment in order to show that any damage on an item of furniture was there before you took it.

5. If you must live above the ground floor make sure any apartment or house you choose has the **views** you want. You might get tired at staring at an alleyway or construction site. Make sure you find out if anything is going to be built nearby in the near future.

Construction projects have a habit of taking a long time, particularly in the developing world. They can also obscure what was formerly a great view.

6. Are the utilities in working order? Do you get hot water from every tap? Is the stove gas or electric? Is the heater adequate? **Air conditioning** may not be available, or may be only available in expensive rentals (Americans may be shocked at this).

7. Find out what **amenities** come with your rental. Do you get access to a gym, a pool, or garden? Are these requirements for any place you might move into?

8. Ask neighbors about their experiences in the neighborhood, or if you choose an apartment, their experiences in the building. Are repairs done on time? What is the general state of the building and area?

Where should I rent?

It all depends on what you can afford, and perhaps more importantly, what you are **comfortable** with. If you decide to live among expats, you will pay more, often significantly more. When I lived in Bahrain, I chose to live not in an expat neighborhood, but with locals in order to save money. I lived in a villa on a dirt road. While I paid less and had much more room than most expats, I was away from the city center and away from native English speakers. I was also nearer to scenes of occasional popular unrest by rioters. It could be uncomfortable, though Bahrain is largely a safe country.

If you live with locals in a developing country, you experience some of the same **challenges** they will experience. The same could be said for living in a rural part of a developed country. It might be a shock you are unused to.

Real Estate

Weigh the pros and cons of expenses versus being comfortable with your surroundings.

You may not have an option **at all**. If you do not speak the local language you won't be able to find more affordable listings in newspapers or other periodicals that are written in the **local language**. Real estate listings in English that cater to expats will always be more expensive than the listings that cater to locals.

The lease agreement might not protect you

A lease agreement has varying degrees of legal protection depending on what country you choose to live in. I'm not an expert in the legal systems of every country, but in my experience living overseas, the more developed the country, the more rights the tenant has. In a lease agreement you should make sure that there is a clause in the agreement that prevents the owner from **selling the property without giving you adequate notice**. Again, some jurisdictions may require an owner to give you first rights to buy the property, some may not allow the owner to throw you out before the lease period ends, and some countries may not enforce tenant rights at all. The poorer and more corrupt the country you move to, the greater the likelihood that the owner of the property you rent will seek to sell it if property values rise considerably. At that point you become a liability.

If a country has a corrupt or incompetent legal system, getting recourse to prevent being thrown out, or to prevent being forced to pay for damages you didn't do is unlikely. The lease agreement will carry little weight. As a retiree expat you will find that time is on the landowner's side, not yours.

However, when entering into a lease agreement, you should go over the terms carefully to determine if there is anything unfair or unrealistic. If you rent a furnished apartment, make sure that all furniture items are listed in the agreement. Make sure you determine how often you can have guests over and whether you can sublease at all. Are pets allowed? Which bills are you responsible for and which bills is the owner responsible for? What date is the rent due?

Can insurance protect me?

Americans have recently had a tough time getting insurance to pay out after a disaster, namely the Katrina hurricane of 2005. Do you think that after a hurricane has blasted through your Caribbean neighborhood insurance companies will pick up the tab for you? **Probably not**.

While I cannot analyze in this book the quality of housing in every developing county that retirees move to, I think it is safe to say as a general rule that the quality is not on par with the first world. That doesn't mean you can't live in a wonderful home, it just means that in the case of a fire or earthquake, your home is unlikely to be able to withstand as much damage as a comparable home in the developed world. One of the leading causes of death in earthquakes in emerging economies is **poor home construction**. In 2010, a magnitude 7.0 earthquake in Haiti killed over 230,000 people. An earthquake of nearly the same magnitude in 1989 in the San Francisco Bay area killed 63 people. While it is unlikely you will retire to a country as poor as Haiti, you will probably retire to a country poorer than your own, and the number killed by any disaster will be considerable.

People who recommend buying property

When doing research on buying property abroad, I strongly suggest ignoring anyone who recommends it as an investment, or recommends it all. I believe I've laid out a very strong argument as to why you **shouldn't** buy property abroad. What do you have to gain that renting won't give you as well? There are many benefits to living abroad, but many drawbacks too. Minimize the latter by not buying property, and be aware of anyone who says it's a "great deal", and "safe". History moves quickly in emerging economies, and so does the value of property.

Beware the unlicensed real estate agent

When dealing with a real estate agent in a foreign country, demand to see the agent's license. If the agent does not have one or reassures you that his license is back in the office or somewhere else, **run – don't walk – away.** Unlicensed real estate agents are a surefire way to buy a property **without a clear title**. This is probably the biggest problem expats face in the purchase of property. While even a licensed real estate agent can give you a property that lacks a clear title, you can bet an unscrupulous con artist with no right to be selling property couldn't care less if he sells you property that is rightfully held by an orphanage. The other thing to be worried about: many unlicensed real estate agents aren't locals, **but fellow westerners**. Find someone who is happy with his home purchase and ask for a recommendation as to which estate agent to use. Don't find one on your own.

Of course if you are going to buy property in a country where real estate agents are not licensed at all, I wish you good luck. You'll need it!

Lack of clear title

As I mentioned previously, lack of clear title is the **biggest issue** facing homeowners abroad. Title disputes are common in every country, but in countries that have only recently allowed expats to buy land, or are opening up a new section of the country to foreign investment, title issues are commonplace. Remember, the legal system, particularly in the developing world, tends to offer no recourse or solution for you unless you are willing to bribe your way to victory. And even then the wheels of "justice" will move exquisitely slowly.

Building and repairs will take forever

If you've ever worked with a contractor or building supervisor in the West, you can imagine that in the developing world, or abroad anywhere you don't speak the local language, the challenges will be immense. Any repairs that will be done, and you can rest assured that repairs will need to be done, will be **time-consuming**, and possibly costly. The expats that I know who have had to wait for a villa or apartment to be constructed have all told me that if they had to do it over again, they **wouldn't** build new.

What about buying property as an investment in the developed world?

While many of the warnings I have given you concerning buying property in the developing world are less relevant in the developed world, even in places like **Spain, Portugal** and **Florida** you see much of the same volatility in housing prices. In any area that is reliant on new home construction and tourism, the local economy is one of feast or famine, depending on the state of the world economy.

Real Estate

The problem with buying a property in places you think are safer and more developed is that you will be **more inclined** to view your property as an investment. But rapid fluctuations in housing prices will ruin any investment possibilities and have other nasty side effects. An article in the British paper, the *Guardian*, from July 24, 2009, entitled "End of the Dream for British Expats in Spain," describes the aftermath of a severe housing crash in Spain for British expats:

"For some, Spain has become a nightmare. Judy and Bill are going back to the West Country this month. Both served in the armed forces, then ran a fish-and-chip shop before coming to a rented villa with a swimming pool and views of the beautiful Jalón Valley in northern Alicante. That was two years ago. Frustration, boredom and their own naked prejudice are driving them home. Encounters with Spanish housing developers and their British estate agents – who scare them so much they do not want their real names used – have left them bitter. 'This is a country with no law,' proclaims Judy. 'We in England abide by the rules but here they don't bother. Even the Brits here rip you off. I think most people would go back if they could. It'll be a relief to get home. It's not as cheap as people think.'"

The fact that you might have chosen a country with a **stronger economy** than say a Latin American or Southeast Asian one can be a double-edged sword. In the wake of the Great Recession, the pound weakened against the Euro, making Spain more much more expensive for British expats, particularly those who were living on pensions that paid in pounds. The *Guardian* article goes on to describe an enormous number of vacant houses in the small seaside towns that were largely populated by British retirees. As vacant developments become eyesores, real estate prices will sink further.

The Financial Guide to Retiring Abroad

Chapter Two – Currencies and Foreign Economies

One of the best ways to determine whether economic trouble is nearby for a country is to look at the price of **credit default swaps (CDS)** for a country's sovereign bond or debt. A CDS is a sort of insurance policy against the default of the bond. When the issuer of a bond defaults, if the bond owner also owns a CDS on the bond, the company that issued the CDS would pay him for his loss.

Credit default swap prices and the likelihood of sovereign default

The **more expensive** the CDS is, the more likely the market and the insurer see the bond as likely to default. As of May 2010, the countries with the most expensive CDS were Venezuela, Argentina, and then Greece. The country with the cheapest CDS? The United States of America. The USA is normally viewed by global markets as the most economically stable country. Recent turmoil in the European Union proves this. If there is any currency you must bet on, bet on the US dollar.

If you are a westerner, particularly an American, you must realize that any country you move to will be less stable economically. Countries with high CDS prices are **the most likely to default**. A default results in (usually) an International Monetary Fund bailout, and severe cuts in government services. The reaction of the populace is almost always protests and possibly rioting. If you move to a country like Argentina, and Argentina's government defaults on its debt, or restructures its debt (which in many ways is simply another form of default) you can fully expect **turmoil** to ensue.

By turmoil I don't necessarily mean full revolution, though that is certainly possible. I mean what we have seen in Greece in 2010: massive rioting, burning buildings, and some deaths. These are more **common** occurrences in countries with fiscally irresponsible governments. Fiscally irresponsible governments are more likely to be found in the developing world, as well as in southern Europe.

For an expat moving to a more **affordable** country the old maxim applies: you get what you pay for. When you move to a country that is extremely affordable, like Argentina, Portugal, Spain, or Vietnam (all countries with high cost CDS for their sovereign debt), while you can expect to live a calm and peaceful existence most of the time, there is always a lurking **possibility** of civil unrest. The civil unrest occurs because the first thing a government does when it cannot pay off its creditors is to either tax its citizens more aggressively, or to cut services that they depend on.

The cutting of services will mean **furloughs** or outright **firing** of government employees. It will mean pension cuts for their retirees (this won't affect you, obviously, as a foreigner), and it may mean hospital services will receive cuts. (This may very well affect you!) All in all, it leads to instability.

My purpose in all this is to hammer home the point that there is no such thing as a free lunch. Many countries irresponsibly allow their economies to run on credit. The Greek government literally lied in its accounting and told the European Union that its deficit was far lower than it actually was. The era of Greece living well beyond its means came to a **sudden** and **undignified** end. Retirees living there were caught in the middle.

Take into consideration the financial stability of the country you are thinking about moving to. By looking at CDS prices before you choose to move there, or at least keeping track of them as you live in your new country, you will have probably the **best** tool to measure your new country's immediate future. If things get rough, you may need to leave in a hurry, or at least prepare for a period of **austerity** and popular anger against the government.

Currency devaluation and what it might mean for you

One of the potential problems in moving abroad is the risk of currency devaluation. **Any country in the world** has the potential to have this problem, though it is far more likely to occur in the developing world where fiscal discipline on the part of the local government is far less than in the developed world. That being said, even the most responsible countries have seen their currencies collapse and a default or devaluation on their debt obligations occur. **Iceland** in 2009 is the most obvious example.

When a country devalues its currency, it is essentially **printing more money** in order to pay its debts. Historically, that meant that the country would go into **hyperinflation** and the country's currency would become all but worthless. The most famous example that comes to mind is the **Weimar Republic,** which was the name of Germany's government before WWII. Germany printed more money to pay off its enormous debts to the other European powers and the United States, as a result of its losing the First World War. A more recent example is that of **Zimbabwe**. In both examples the governments felt compelled to print money to pay off enormous debts. Both efforts were **unsuccessful** and led to scenes of people pushing wheelbarrows filled with worthless currency in order to buy basic items.

Hyperinflation **destroys** the savings of everyone in the country. If the government creates a new currency to stem hyperinflation, the result **permanently** wipes out people's savings. This will obviously have an effect on not only the country's citizens, but residents, such as expats, as well.

In today's world, hyperinflation is a rarity. But it is still possible, as Zimbabwe has shown. For most countries under the threat of hyperinflation or default, there is an organization of last resort that will usually issue loans in **dollars** for a country to pay its debts. That organization is the **International Monetary Fund (IMF).**

Currencies and Foreign Economies

The most recent example of a country defaulting on its debt is Iceland. Before the current financial crisis, Iceland was viewed by many as one of the best countries in the world to live in. Its high standard of living was due in large part to its financial sector, which made up a considerable part of the country's economy. The Icelandic financial sector became **indebted** to other financial institutions around the world, and when a **credit crunch** occurred, all of Iceland's banks were unable to pay their depositors or creditors.

The result was that Iceland's entire financial system collapsed. For our purposes, the experience of retail depositors in Iceland's banking system is important to look at. Virtually all accounts were **frozen**, and depositors were unable to get to their money. Many people from around the world had put their money in Icelandic banks because of the appearance of Iceland as a **stable** country with very high rates of interest on savings accounts. Now, with the credit crunch in full force, Iceland's bank accounts appeared to be a deal **too good to be true**.

Iceland's Krona overnight threatened to become worthless, and only an enormous bailout package from both the IMF and a large number of European nations saved the currency and Iceland's banking system. But for those who invested in Iceland and deposited in its banks, there were moments of doubt as to whether they would get everything they invested back.

Many Europeans had invested in Icelandic banks under programs such as **Icesave** which gave far higher than market-average interest rates for deposit accounts. Banks in the developing world **routinely** offer depositors higher than average interest rates in order to attract customers.

The Financial Guide to Working Overseas

Never put your money in these accounts. Banks abroad are rarely insured by their governments and if they fail, your money goes with them.

It is also a common con for a criminal to set up a sort of **Ponzi scheme** by creating a bank and then offering high interest rates on accounts. Allen Stanford, an American, founded a bank in the country of Antigua and Barbuda known as the Bank of Antigua. The bank offered customers too-good-to-be-true returns on their accounts, and when the market went into recession, depositors' money disappeared. Stanford is in prison now, but his customers' money is gone. Remember if it seems **too good to be true it probably is**. Keep your money in banks back home that are guaranteed to return your money if they go under.

The best way to protect yourself from currency devaluation is to have most of your money **kept in a stable currency**. What currencies are stable? **The most stable currency in the world is the US dollar, followed by the Euro, then the Japanese yen, and finally the Swiss franc, in that order.** My reasoning for this is that these are the most popular currencies in descending order held by the world's various central banks as **currency reserves**. As of 2009, the U.S. dollar makes up approximately 61.5 per cent of the world's currency reserves. The dollar is so popular a currency with all of the world's governments that it is known as the world's reserve currency. Many commodities are officially priced in dollars, most famously oil. The dollar's status as the world's reserve currency allows the US to run up huge trade deficits indefinitely, and suffer few if any repercussions. Whether this can last forever is another story.

Currencies and Foreign Economies

You will hear periodically that the dollar is on its way out, or that the Euro is going to take the lead. Many countries who dislike the United States' domination of world finance will occasionally make announcements that they are trying to find an alternative to holding huge sums of dollars in their central banks. **Ignore them**. They are just complaining, and nothing more. There is no currency on the horizon that has the backing of a powerful nation behind it to take the place of the dollar. For those Americans living abroad who are thinking of abandoning their own currency for another, think again. The **foreign exchange market (FX)** does the vast majority of its trading in one currency only, the US dollar, to the tune of well over 80 per cent of trades. The market believes the dollar is the currency of choice. Shouldn't you?

While the Euro is growing in popularity, as of 2010, with the crisis surrounding Greece and that country's risk of default, you can see that the only true safe currency in the world is the almighty US dollar. That is not to say that this will be the case forever. All empires fall, as do all reserve currencies. But until the European Union gives its Central Bank the same powers that the United States' Federal Reserve has over its currency, you can expect periodic shocks to the value of the Euro.

That is not to say that the Euro is not a great currency to have your money in. I believe, based on the popularity of certain currencies as currency reserves, and the popularity of currencies traded, that there are about twelve currencies that a person can confidently store their money in. Those currencies are in descending order of safety: US dollar, Euro, Japanese yen, Pound sterling, Swiss franc, Australian dollar, Canadian dollar, Swedish kroner, Hong Kong dollar, Norwegian krone, New Zealand dollar, Singapore dollar. The top six are very stable. All of these countries have shown pretty strong **fiscal responsibility** for decades. Yes, there are occasional bouts with inflation, but nothing unreasonable.

My advice for an expat coming from the developed world and moving to the developing world is to keep the **bulk of your money** in your own currency at all times. Avoid putting substantial amounts of money in the local currency. Developing world currencies are **weak** and volatile and periodically become inflated and worthless. Having the bulk of your money in dollars, Euros, pounds etc. will keep your money far safer. While the currencies of the developed world can suffer from inflation as well, they are being managed by far more fiscally responsible leaders than those of the developing world.

However, if you are moving from one **developed** country to another for your retirement, you should **convert** as much of your portfolio as possible to your new home's currency **if you plan on retiring to that new country**. Why? If you have retired to France from the United States for instance, and are dependent on an investor portfolio that is primarily in dollars, if the dollar goes through a period of inflation your budget will be hit hard! That means replacing US savings bonds, which as an expat you should primarily be invested in, into various European bonds, primarily from the strongest and most stable economies in the Euro-zone: France and/or Germany.

In the long run, the Euro and the pound will always be stronger currencies than the dollar. The British and EU Central Banks have embarked on long-term strategies to make this so. That means that whether you are a citizen of those countries, or are moving into them, adjust your expenses accordingly. If you come from a weaker currency like the US dollar, you will always find that your currency buys less in those countries than at home. I expect this to stay this way **indefinitely.** If there are dramatic changes in the way things work, expect them to be discussed in future editions!

Conversely, you can also expect countries with smaller economies, or countries that are poorer, to have currencies of less value. So expect a Mexican peso to be worth less than a dollar or Euro, and a Canadian dollar and an Australian dollar to be near parity with the US dollar. Every central bank in the world wants to keep these exchange rates as constant as possible, because to do otherwise means to risk inflation.

Having a currency worth less is **not** a sign of a weak economy, nor is having a currency worth more a sign of a strong economy. It is simply the monetary policy of those respective countries. Budget for it, but **don't worry** too much about it. The relative values are **usually arbitrary.** Exchange rates are set by central banks and are kept as constant as possible to prevent inflation, the greatest fiscal fear of every government.

Is the Euro stable?

One of the big questions to come out of this most recent global financial crisis is the stability of the Euro. Several countries in the Eurozone, including Greece, Spain, and Ireland, face the prospect of defaulting on their debt. The Euro is seen by some as a mistake.

I believe the Euro is a stable currency. However, the governmental structure of the European Union makes it a **federal** system similar to the United States. How is that relevant to default? The United States has **never defaulted** on its foreign debt, that is, the money it owes to foreign creditors through bonds and other Treasury-backed securities. But the states and cities within the United States **regularly default**. Currently California and Colorado have or are considering renegotiating the pensions of their state government employees, which could certainly be considered a form of default.

European countries within the Euro-zone are essentially **states**. Like states in America they issue their own bonds. But without the means to print their own currency, and because they are dependent on the currency of a European Central Bank like the Federal Reserve of the United States, they will be put into indebted positions like American states such as California, Colorado etc. This means they will most likely default more often than they have in the past.

However, the European Union as a whole will be a **reliable** entity. This is just my opinion, but I believe it is an opinion backed up by historical fact. The EU is facing its worst financial crisis in its short history, yet the calls for it to be broken up are on the fringe. Europe will survive and move forward, but countries within it will either default outright, renegotiate their debts, and/or take severe **austerity** measures to attempt to pay their debts and balance budgets.

You as a potential retiree to Europe should be aware that the country you are in may be individually more unstable, but **collectively** Europe as a whole is safer. The financial instability that came from the Great Depression and in some ways led to Fascism I do not believe will return. But the price for that general stability will be more regional fiscal instability in Europe, as the American experience demonstrates.

Currencies and Foreign Economies

Which currencies are vulnerable?

Because all currencies are no longer backed by a precious metal such as gold or silver, in a sense all currencies are vulnerable to declining in value or becoming worthless. But what makes a country's currency actually lose value? In my opinion the **fiscal policy** of a currency's government is in part to blame. Countries with easy access to credit and that have a history of balanced budgets are far less likely to default or to jeopardize the value of their currency.

According to the book *This Time is Different*, a landmark study of countries and their histories of sovereign default, there are essentially two tiers of countries. There are countries that default periodically, and there are more evolved countries (almost always Western countries) that rarely if ever default. Currencies in the first group are not to be trusted.

What are the odds of default?

If you move to a developing country, the chances that that country will default at some point during your stay there are **very high.** Historically, almost every country in the world has defaulted on its foreign debt, and devalued its currency as a consequence. In fact, according to *This Time is Different*, only six countries have never defaulted on their foreign debt: the United States, New Zealand, Australia, Canada, Thailand and Denmark.

That is a very short list, and there are 185 other countries in the world. Developing countries default regularly, rarely going more than thirty years without a currency devaluation to pay off debts. When a country allows its financial sector to go unregulated and to borrow too much, or when a country's government itself borrows too much money, a default and devaluation is sure to follow. Developing countries will also default with far lower amounts of debt than developed countries. Countries like the United States can borrow far higher amounts of money in relation to GDP than a developing country can, with no fear of default. The market has no confidence in a poor country's ability to pay off debt, so interest rates on loans to poor countries are usually much higher than to rich countries.

All of this stresses the point that you should keep as much of your money in your **home currency** as possible, and keep it in banks in your home country. The more money you have in local currency, the more that will be wiped out when a devaluation occurs. If you have most of your money in your home currency, you will be largely unscathed when default comes.

This is also another reason **not to buy property abroad**. Buying property abroad is essentially converting a large part of your money that is in a stable currency, into an asset that is valued in an unstable currency. If there is a local default, you will not be able to sell your house to local buyers, and will only be able to find buyers who are foreign expats like you. You may not think this is a problem, but any time you are selling a property and have lost a large chunk of potential buyers, it can make selling a nightmare.

Dollar denominated currencies

Currently, there are **nine** countries and territories that use the dollar outside the United States and **three** countries and territories that use the Euro. Other countries maintain one-to-one convertibility between the dollar and their local currency. Developing countries have long struggled with having nearly worthless currencies in which foreign investors and creditors refuse to do business. Some countries have taken it upon themselves to adopt two of the strongest and most stable currencies in the world, the dollar and the Euro, in order to grow their economy and add stability.

In the interim, if you are a developing country and you adopt a stable currency like the dollar, you are doing a lot to convince your citizens to have confidence in your economy and financial institutions. However, there are many **risks** involved with adopting a foreign and more stable currency that you do not yourself **print**.

One of the biggest risks is that if the country that uses a foreign currency, or maintains strict convertibility, gets too deeply into debt, it will **default** and not be able to pay off creditors. This happened to Argentina in 2002. The then government of Argentina had convinced itself that linking one-to-one to the more fiscally responsible American economy would result in stability. However, the adoption of the dollar link only covered up the Argentine government's inability to control its excessive borrowing.

Below are the countries in the developing world that have adopted the Euro or the dollar as their own currency.

Countries and territories that use the Euro outside the Euro-zone:

1. Akrotiri and Dhekelia
2. Kosovo
3. Montenegro

Countries and territories that use the US dollar outside the United States:

1. British Virgin Islands

2. East Timor
3. Ecuador
4. El Salvador
5. Marshall Islands
6. Micronesia
7. Palau
8. Panama
9. Turks and Caicos Islands

Other countries have intermittently linked their currencies to the dollar and Euro through a **peg**. Below are the countries and territories currently pegging their currency to the dollar:

1. Aruba
2. Bahamas
3. Bahrain
4. Barbados
5. Bermuda
6. Cayman Islands
7. China
8. Cuba
9. East Caribbean Dollar countries (Antigua and Barbuda, Dominica, Grenada, Saint Kitts and Nevis, Saint Lucia, Saint Vincent and the Grenadines, Anguilla, Montserrat)
10. Djibouti
11. Eritrea
12. Hong Kong
13. Macau
14. Kuwait (pegged to several stable currencies including the dollar)

Currencies and Foreign Economies

15. Lebanon
16. Maldives
17. Oman
18. Netherland Antilles (Curacao and Bonaire)
19. Qatar
20. Saudi Arabia
21. United Arab Emirates
22. Venezuela

Countries and territories whose currencies are pegged to the Euro:

1. Benin
2. Burkina Faso
3. Bulgaria
4. Cote d'Ivoire (Ivory Coast)
5. Cape Verde
6. Comoros
7. Cameroon
8. Central African Republic
9. Chad
10. Republic of Congo
11. Denmark
12. Equatorial Guinea
13. Gabon
14. Guinea Bissau
15. French Polynesia
16. New Caledonia
17. Wallis and Futuna
18. Mali

19. Niger
20. Senegal
21. Togo

You will notice that much of the Caribbean is linked to other currencies. Recently the Cayman Islands, famous as a center of money laundering and as a tax haven, was told by the British government to start taxing its residents and those who conduct business there in order to raise money. The Caymans cannot print more money because of their peg, and because they do not have taxes cannot raise revenue that way. Instead their only source of money in a time of crisis is to beg the British government, their owner, for a loan. **Beware of tax havens and territories whose currencies are pegged to others**. What seems safe and stable can collapse at any moment.

The major risk in linking your currency to a stronger one is that if you fall deeply into debt and tax revenues fall because of a recession, you will be unable to pay your debts. A government in this position will then panic and cut services (government jobs, renegotiate pensions, cut government projects such as bridges and buildings etc.) and in a final step issue a new currency or declare that the current currency is worth a different value. The people of the country react by protesting and rioting as their savings are destroyed.

So don't fool yourself that you are moving to a more stable country because that country has adopted the dollar or the Euro. Catastrophe is certainly a possibility, if the government of the country you moved to decides to print more money to pay off debts. The currency peg that once meant stability was simply a temporary illusion.

Currencies and retirement

I am assuming that when you save your money, you are investing for retirement or saving for the purchase of a home. The problem with being a long term expat and investing for retirement is that if you are not making enough money, you will be precluded from retiring wherever you want. Throughout your career you should seek to earn as much as possible and **save** as much as possible; only in this way will you have enough for retirement.

The problem with saving and investing as an expat is that it can be difficult to decide **which** currency to save your money in. My basic rule of thumb is this: **if you wish to retire in a developed country save your money in the currency of the country you plan to retire in. If you wish to retire to the developing world, save your money in either dollars, Euros, or another developed currency with a good outlook**.

As you can see, it is essential for an expat to have as high a salary as possible throughout his or her career in order to be able to return home to retire. As I am assuming that the people reading this book are from the developed world, I am assuming that the people reading this book are from countries with high costs of living. That means that a career spent in a developing country earning a relatively low salary will **doom** you to never retiring back home, as the amount you will have saved in investments will never cover your expenses in retirement.

Unfortunately, I am asking an expat to essentially **predict the future**. However, I am not asking you to predict anyone's future but your own. Saving money in the currency of the country where you plan on retiring, or at least in a developed-country currency, means avoiding any possible large **currency devaluations** and makes sure that your investments don't become worthless in the future, particularly if they are in cash and bonds. That is why it is essential for an expat to have a vague idea of where he or she will settle later in life.

As you work, you should convert your savings for retirement immediately into the currency of the country you plan on retiring in. You can do this by doing the conversion and putting the money in a bank account of that denominated in that currency or by investing in equities and bonds from that country's economy. By doing the conversion as you earn the money and keeping the money in that currency over the long run, you reduce your exposure to currency fluctuations over time. You only have to deal with currency exchange issues once, at the first moment when you convert the money and invest it.

The problem of which currency to put your money into creeps up when you live in a developing country and are forced to choose the currency of your home country for your retirement investments. In this scenario you are hoping that the country you are working in does not become developed itself and become expensive to live in, relative to your home country. I do believe that while this scenario is theoretically possible, it is unlikely. It takes decades for a country to become developed and have a currency with a high value, and it is also unlikely that we will see a developed country default on its debt by printing money. But again, anything is possible, and it is a key risk to having a career in the developing world.

Chapter Three – Your career abroad

For the vast majority of expats who move abroad to work, the goal is an immediate **increase in salary**, as opposed to a long term career boost. In a foreign corporation, an expat is typically viewed as an outsider who will help professionalize the middle manager or lower executive ranks. He or she **is not a person who will be viewed as someone to run the company.**

If you think about it, how many large companies have foreign CEOs? Certainly, the number is increasing year by year, but the vast majority of businesses have a local citizen as the head of the company, rather than a foreigner. In parts of the world, such as Europe, where companies are slowly coming to be seen as multi-national rather than anchored to one nation, it is more likely that you will see foreign heads of companies. But in most of the world, and the developing world in particular, the heads of companies are still usually **native-born**.

That means that there is a **glass ceiling** for an expat. You can only rise so far in your career and many expats come to this realization soon in their time abroad. The most ambitious expats might return home and try to get to the top in their home country. But many will stay abroad, and simply be content with their larger salary and exotic locale.

Should you move abroad for more money?

I feel you should **only** move abroad for more money, unless of course you are committed to working overseas for a non-profit whose main purpose is in the area of development and fighting poverty. From a financial perspective, moving abroad for more money is the only move that makes sense. Why? When you move abroad you frequently are not making contributions to your state pension. The longer you work abroad for less pay, the longer you are not making contributions, which will leave you in quite a bind when it is time to retire.

This is an enormous issue when it comes to moving abroad to the developing world. In most developing countries, the pay is lower, and there is no program to help you put money toward your pension. If you move between developed countries this is less of an issue because they will either be using the same currency (Euro to Euro), or another strong currency (Euro to dollar). Since you will probably be paid a high salary, your contributions to your state pension or retirement plan will be satisfactory

If you are moving abroad because a company is posting you abroad, you probably won't have any issues either. The problems result when you work for local companies in your new country. They will typically not have any programs set up that will allow you to contribute to your state pension. **That means you must save substantial portions of your income to make up for the shortfall**. You must also invest these portions wisely in safe investments. I'll talk later about how to invest wisely for retirement.

Many expats who move to the developing world in places like Dubai or Hong Kong do so for a higher salary. However, they make the mistake of not saving for retirement and not making contributions to their home country's pension plan. They use their higher salary to instead improve their lifestyle. That means more going out, more drinking, and generally more excessive spending. I've lived this way myself, and it means no savings for retirement.

As an expat in the developing world you must be **disciplined** and save substantial portions of your income (at least 10 per cent per annum). Otherwise you may face problems in retirement. When you live abroad, you will most likely not be contributing to your home country's pension system. The lack of contributions will mean less for you in retirement. Thus it is extremely important that you save large parts of your income in order to make up the difference.

In the developing world this problem is **magnified**. You are probably going to earn less money in developing countries, and what money you earn will be in a currency that is probably not highly valued. The longer you live in poorer countries with a lower salary relative to what you could be earning in a developed country, the more money you are neglecting to invest for your retirement. If you miss out too much in making large contributions to your retirement plan, you won't be able to retire where you want to in the world, and you may have to permanently make do in a part of the world that has a low cost of living.

Experience and working overseas

Generally, it is very difficult to find work overseas if you lack experience. Most of the work for expats requires experience. Employers are not looking to train an expat; they are looking for someone who can hit the ground running. Expats are commonly viewed as professionals who will add something extra to an organization, something an organization cannot get locally. Training an expat for an entry level position doesn't make sense when you take into account the expense of flying an expat out for a position and paying them a higher salary than is typical locally.

Two types of expats

There are basically two types of expats. The first type of expat is hired because he or she is cheap labor. If the expat is male, he can be anything from a bricklayer to a taxi driver to a waiter to an office administrator. If female, she can be anything from a prostitute to a housekeeper to a waitress to an office secretary. This is the brutal truth. Most of these expats are from poor countries that are known for sending many of their citizens abroad. Many countries are utterly dependent on expats for **remittances** (money sent back home to families) so much so that large percentages of a country's GDP can come from this money.

Countries that source these expats include India, the Philippines, Ethiopia, Russia, Ukraine, Mexico and Pakistan. Because South Asian nations and the Philippines were former colonies of English speaking nations, their citizens have learned English as a second language (if they are educated). Their expats are in demand as office staff to answer phones and communicate with native English speakers. When I lived in the Persian Gulf, a part of the world utterly dependent on expat labor, most expats came from South Asia and the Philippines. Since Arabic is hardly spoken outside the Arab world, Arabs have compromised and learned English and thus make an effort to recruit expats who also speak this language.

This book is not for this type of expat. This type of expat is usually treated **horrendously**, has few if any legal rights (almost none if he or she is illegally residing in the country), and works in deplorable conditions. Many female expats of this type are basically victims of **sex traffickers** and work the nightclubs and bars in the more popular expat locales.

The second type of expat is **you.** This expat goes overseas for adventure and/or for significantly higher pay, is typically a holder of a **western passport** and is free to move whenever he or she pleases. The first type of expat commonly has his or her passport confiscated and is in effect an indentured servant.

My point in writing this is to hammer home the true function of being an expat: **adventure** or **higher pay**. Adventure is typically of short duration, and more for younger expats. Higher pay is essential for everyone else. Do not accept a job until you have **written confirmation** of what you are being compensated, and make sure that it is significantly higher (at least 15 per cent) than what you are currently making in your home country. Otherwise, it is generally not worth it to take the job (unless you are desperate which is another matter altogether).

Salary and compensation expectations

As I stated before, you must make sure that your salary is going up considerably before taking a job abroad. If you have a family, the company **should** offer you, at a minimum, drastically reduced tuition for your children at the best private schools your children can gain entrance to. This is a standard package for an expat, particularly in the more exotic (read: impoverished) foreign locales.

The more popular locales for expats such as Hong Kong, Dubai, and Singapore may or may not have companies that offer your children free or reduced tuition at private schools. Because most expats want to work in these locations, companies do not have to go out of their way to attract talent. To offset the cost of tuition, you must be paid the highest salary possible. If you cannot afford to send your children to the best schools in the location of your choice, I strongly suggest that you do not choose to work there. If you are single, all of this discussion is of course, pointless.

As an expat you must have **comprehensive healthcare** for you and your entire family. This is essential. Do not take a job offer that does not include this in your compensation package. No reputable firm would offer an expat employee from a developed country a job without healthcare. A **dental plan** is also a consideration. A dental plan is, however, far less expensive than standard health insurance so there is room for negotiating here. However, any executive position should include a dental plan in your compensation package.

When it comes to the **perks** of an overseas posting, the only way to accurately know what to expect is to determine what executives doing your type of work are getting paid in the same locale. Before you take an offer, make sure you find out what can be asked for in a compensation package. In a country with a high cost of living, it may be too much to ask for a car, rent and schooling. In a poorer country, it may be standard. Countries that are very poor are typically labeled as **hardship** postings, and you will be compensated with a higher salary (if you are in a job sector that pays well) and be given associated perks. In more developed countries you will not be paid so well, but you will be able to depend more on the strong infrastructure of those countries (public transportation, free healthcare), and should expect less correspondingly.

When you are selected for a job, you should expect to be given temporary accommodation in a hotel for a period of time until you can find your own housing. This may or may not be deducted partially from your salary. The more reputable the company and higher paid you are, the more likely the hotel stay will be free or largely subsidized.

Compensation in countries which are poor

Some companies will argue that you should not be paid a higher salary because your salary will be far higher than the average salary in the country. I say, **accept these offers at your own risk**. I personally would never accept such an offer. Though you will be making far more than the average impoverished native of that country, you will be making far less than the average native of **your** country.

That means you will be unable to **save** enough money for your retirement back home. Now some of you may be saying that you have no plans to retire back home. **You do not know that**. The vast majority of expats return home, particularly if they work in the developing world. The biggest reason they return home: **healthcare**. When living abroad, your private healthcare is not guaranteed. If you become very ill or are injured badly, your private healthcare may seek to drop your coverage at some point should your treatment become too expensive.

This means that you are utterly dependent on your own country's healthcare system as a backup. If you are ill or injured and have to return home, you may never be able to leave. For this very significant reason, you should never think that you will cut your ties with your home country forever, and you should save accordingly. If you are spending years in poor countries earning a poor wage, it is highly unlikely you will have saved enough to live well if you are forced to move back home.

Three types of overseas private sector employers

There are basically three types of employers for an expat. They are as follows:

1. **A local company.** By that I mean a company that is based and headquartered in the country you plan to move to.
2. **A foreign franchise of a company that is based on where you are from.** Franchising is a huge business overseas, and foreign companies will adopt a well known, usually western, franchise to appear more professional and bigger than they truly are.
3. **A foreign office of a company from your home country or another developed country**. Your working there is probably the result of a temporary transfer from your home country. These kinds of transfers occur when you are on an executive fast track or if you are being exiled out of the company.

I am intimately familiar with the first two, and somewhat familiar with the third. I would argue that the third option is the best option for an expat. You will probably still be able to make contributions to your state pension and to any retirement plans you might have. Your career is still obviously on some sort of track and going overseas is advancing it. You will be working with management that is from your own country and you will not have the culture shock of the first two employer types. Basically, this is a good position to be in.

The second option, where you work for a **franchise,** is a very common option. You may or may not be working closely with managers of your own nationality so there is still the possibility of culture shock. The problem with this kind of job is that while it seems that you are working for a reputable giant company with endless career possibilities, in reality you will be working for a small franchise owner who will run the company as he or she sees fit. Franchises such as this one are very common in the developing world, but also exist in the developed world.

Another issue with working for a franchise is that you are made to assume that you have a close relationship with all the offices in your **network**. You are made to assume this because it is usually a selling point for your job. A young expat will be told in the interview of the potential for being transferred to any location in the world he or she wants if they perform well. This is usually a **lie**. While the franchise will have some connection with the other offices, the transfer of employees is rare. Logically, why would an office transfer away a good employee? You're probably stuck where you work, unless you resign and find work elsewhere.

In terms of career path, you will soon confront the issue of the **glass ceiling** as I have written elsewhere. As you are a foreigner, the ownership or control of the company will typically be given to someone of the same nationality as the current owner, rather than to an expat. You have been selected for your expertise, but it is unlikely that you will be trusted with holding the reins.

The Financial Guide to Working Overseas

There is however, a benefit to working for a franchise, and that is the fact that it will look good on your resume/CV. It is also usually easier to get a job at a franchise office than at that company in its home location. When you apply for other positions in other companies, you will have a work history with the names of some of the world's leading companies. You don't have to be completely honest and tell them it's just a franchise. For all intents and purposes you actually did work for that "name" company.

A **local company** is the worst option for an expat. You don't get the name value of working for a franchise or for a local office. You will undoubtedly work in an office filled with foreign staff which might lead to culture shock. The quality of the expats you work with, if there are any, will be low.

These types of jobs, however, may pay higher than the franchise or even the foreign office options. At the very least, you should demand higher pay for the sacrifices you may be making to your career. You will not be able to brag about your employment here on your resume/CV. And you will most likely lack the perks of working at the other two types of jobs.

Another issue with working abroad is your rights as an expat. If you are depending on a work visa while working abroad, a local company and a franchise can be expected to **mistreat** you if they feel like it. This may mean being fired at any moment and being forced to leave the country in a matter of days or minutes, regardless as to how settled you are in the country. This is particularly a problem in the less developed the country you are working in is.

What do you owe your employer?

When you begin work you should owe your employer **nothing** other than hard work and a professional effort. There may be an arrangement where a portion of your salary is deducted to pay for temporary accommodation until you find your own place. The better the job, the more likely housing will be a part of the package. Certainly the more wild and dangerous the environment, the more generous the package. The more developed the country, the less likely an employer will give you anything as they assume you will easily find housing on your own.

It is a common practice for expats on the lower rungs of the ladder to be indebted to their employers, particularly if they are from poor countries. In the Gulf, millions of laborers from South Asia are deeply indebted to their employers for their housing and travel expenses. This is a common ruse to **enslave** employees indefinitely and get an employer out of having to pay for labor.

If your employer suggests that you owe him for paying for your flight to the country, **immediately leave the job and the country at once**. No respectable employer will charge an employee for being settled in. An employee who is "indebted" to the employer will not be paid, and will work essentially work to pay off the debt. This is illegal in virtually every county, but is often not enforced in poorer parts of the world.

Being indebted to your employer is a dangerous position to be in. As an expat, you often lack rights, and in many countries can be imprisoned for being in debt. Avoid this situation at all costs. If your new employers suggest you owe them a great deal of money for what is a standard move overseas, I would advise you to excuse yourself, run to the airport and never return.

Working overseas for a franchise or local company means that you, the employee, can be fired at any moment and are subject to the whim of the company's ownership. However, in my experience a foreign office of a company from your home country or from another developed country will treat an employee according to the law of its headquarters. In essence, working for such companies will mean being treated as if you are still working in your home country, with only the setting changed. This is obviously an ideal work setting.

The new economy and its impact on expat work

Unfortunately for job seekers, we are in the midst of an almost global economic crisis. That means that those people who were willing to move to another country for new opportunities may not be able to escape unemployment no matter where they move.

That means you may be forced into a job with **reduced benefits**. Schooling for your children may not be paid for. You may not be given a company car. You may not have your housing paid for. In short, you may be just like everyone else.

However, while I stated that the current economic crisis is **almost** global, I did not say it was global. There are still countries, particularly in South America, Oceania and other areas that have remained relatively untouched. There are also war zones, and war zones means government spending and government jobs, however dangerous.

In short I believe you should demand what you feel comfortable demanding. If you have two or more offers on the table, you are negotiating from strength. If you are dependent on one offer you may have to take it. There may not be another opportunity for awhile.

The difficulties of finding work in another country

The greatest difficulty in finding work in another country is that the office where you will work is generally far away. This may make interviewing for a job extremely difficult in some situations.

Countries and territories that are dependent on large numbers of expats for labor such as Dubai, Singapore, Hong Kong, Shanghai, etc. are used to hiring via a phone interview or a quick meeting in a third country. Trying for a country that is not used to large numbers of expats will probably mean that you must temporarily relocate to that country to find work, either under a tourist visa or a highly skilled migrant visa if it is available.

Industries that are dependent on large numbers of expats (including information technology, engineering, mining etc.) will usually have the means to interview potential expats from abroad. These industries know better than to depend on local talent (which may be non-existent) and will make suitable arrangements.

Obviously the worst position to be in is to be an expat in a foreign country looking for work. Because you are in a foreign country, you generally do not have a place to stay and/or a network to help you find a job. If you are on some kind of special visa you may have only a limited time before it **expires** and you have to leave. If you are looking for work on a tourist visa, it may not be legal for you to actually look for work (though this is hard to enforce in most of the world).

In such a situation you need to plan ahead. Remember, an employer does not care where you live as long as you can get to the office on time. Stay at the cheapest accommodation possible. I recommend a hostel, but pay extra for your own room. You will need privacy to collect your thoughts and to stay organized.

Priceline.com, and its Name Your Own Price feature, is a godsend. There is a trick to using this service. Look for a decent starred hotel level, and then name (bid) a very low price. You may not get it, but you will probably get a reasonably priced room at a very nice hotel for literally pennies on the dollar. The hotels do not care. So long as the rooms are filled with paying customers rather than empty, they are OK with losing less money. Be warned though, this option is not available in all parts of the world.

Remember, if you are planning on interviewing for a job in another country, you will have to make arrangements suitable to your schedule. If you are currently unemployed, it won't be an issue, but finding the time to schedule interviews overseas while working in another country can be extremely hectic. How do you make an excuse to travel abroad for several days in order to interview? Many employers understand the issue with interviewing overseas, and final interviews are often conducted over the phone. **But be prepared to fly at a moment's notice**. And make sure you are prepared to make an excuse to your current employer for disappearing for several days.

Working for your government overseas

Virtually every government in the world sends thousands of its citizens abroad to work. The most common work for these individuals is with their countries consulates and embassies. Embassies and consulates are essential to allow countries to maintain relationships with each other, to help their own citizens who are living and working abroad, and to act as meeting and entertainment centers for dignitaries.

Every government has a foreign service of some kind from which they draw the staff necessary to fill roles in the various embassies and consulates around the world. The wealthier the country, the more countries available to work in as the expenses of setting up an embassy, consulate or trade office are extremely high.

Western countries tend to also view their properties overseas as potential targets for terrorists and criminals. It is not uncommon for an embassy or consulate to be the scene of protests (usually staged by the local government to pressure that country). Because of this, many countries have considerable numbers of security personnel guarding their overseas properties. American embassies and consulates are generally built like fortresses and have several layers of security. Anyone planning on working overseas for an American government body should expect to deal regularly with large amounts of local security.

With all that being said, you can expect as a government employee to generally be treated fairly, and to have your employment rights respected. Working in a consulate or embassy or other government office in a foreign country can be dangerous, and you may be eligible for additional hazard pay, but this will vary from government to government and by location abroad. You should also expect your housing to be paid for as part of your compensation package.

The Financial Guide to Working Overseas

Based on my conversations with government workers overseas, the type of work varies depending on the needs of that government's expats living there, and the relationship of the foreign country with the home country. **The closer the relationship, the larger the presence.** In Dubai, the British have an "embassy" (though Dubai is not a separate country it is treated as such) and their presence is considerably larger than the American presence which is simply some office space in a building. The reason for this is that there are many more British citizens living in Dubai than Americans, and the British government has deemed it necessary to have a large presence there in order to maintain its closer relationship with Dubai and to serve its own citizens better.

Another type of work that is commonly found overseas is that of **government contractors**. Governments have worked to privatize many of their functions overseas for a variety of reasons. The most controversial use of government contractors has been as **mercenaries**. While mercenaries are generally paid more than their government soldier counterpart, they are also more expendable and most likely do not have access to the resources their government counterparts have. An expat should have military experience before applying for these roles.

Governments that outsource positions also outsource the hiring, so an applicant may very well be working to forward a government's goals in a region, but be answering entirely to a private sector boss and hierarchy. Private companies that have won government contracts will not just hire westerners for high salaries. They will also be looking to the developing world for unskilled or semi-skilled labor. When applying for these types of jobs, I would recommend looking for the highest salary possible, as low paid positions will be for potentially dangerous and unskilled work.

Those looking for the same guarantees and benefits that one would find in a government position should look elsewhere. There is a profit motive for the company that is setting up the work and to make a profit something has to be cut. That means all the guarantees and access to resources will not be there. You are in the private sector when you work as a government contractor. There may however be many of the same **security requirements** and **background checks** that are part of government work. Government contractors may be higher paid in some cases, but if they are working on sensitive materials alongside government employees, they will be forced to qualify for the same security clearances as anyone in the government.

Working in a war zone

War is a lucrative business. It remains the most obvious example of government spending and waste, and it can result in death and destruction on a massive scale.

It can however, result in employment opportunities for thousands. When I lived in the Middle East, the Iraq war was at its height, and on a weekly basis thousands of American military personnel could be seen visiting the local malls of Dubai where I lived, spending portions of their income on the latest electronic gadgets for sale at the Mall of the Emirates.

Not all of these men and women were soldiers. Many were contract employees, NGO workers, US and British government staff dedicated to organizing the logistics of the military efforts in Iraq and Afghanistan. War remains an enormous effort, particularly if led by a giant world power like the United States, and as a result of that, thousands upon thousands of employees of all kinds are needed to support the effort.

Many countries now view war as something that the private sector can do better than the public sector. This is particularly true of the United States. I have seen firsthand that the US government's efforts to privatize various aspects of war have allowed companies to be established that can field armies larger than many countries' own militaries.

What about the danger? From discussing with friends who have worked in war zones, I believe that while danger is all around you and can strike at any moment, the moments of actual danger are few and far between. **That doesn't mean that it is safe to work in such an environment**. In fact it is extremely risky. Work in war zones is boredom punctuated by quick moments of extreme terror that can result in your death or serious injury.

For most expats working in war zones, the actual battles of the war will be occurring far away in the countryside. Most expats will do their work in cities and never see the enemy (particularly if it is a guerrilla war), and will go about their daily business unaware of action occurring miles away. For expats working in NGOs and other organizations that do work on the battlefield and in the countryside, war will be a great deal closer at hand. Expats in these roles are captured regularly for both ransom and to make a political statement. The latter event usually means death for the expat captured.

The job interview

As an expat interested in working overseas you should prepare as you would for any normal job interview. That will mean gaining as much knowledge of the company as possible, presenting yourself in the most professional manner possible (well dressed, suit and tie etc.), and coming to the interview on time. A job interview for a foreign position should be the same as a job interview for a domestically-based position.

There is of course an **exception**. Your interview may very well be conducted abroad and will require you to travel. A reputable firm will make every effort to either interview you in person **and pay for the cost to do so if you must travel to interview**. Never travel to a far off country on your money. If a company wishes to see you in person and see how you interact in their environment they should pay for you to come over. You can expect a company that has little respect for its employees to ask that you pay for yourself.

For entry level positions it is not uncommon for a foreign company to hire someone simply on the basis of a telephone interview. I have been hired this way, but the position I was hired for was certainly not an executive level position. Any company that is willing to pay you a salary of six figures or higher will fly you to the interview location at no charge.

When you are flown out, if it is required for you to stay overnight, the company interviewing you should pay for the hotel stay. Feel free to judge the quality of the hotel and in so doing judge the quality of the company that is considering hiring you. A reputable company will select for you at least a three star, and preferably a four star hotel that caters to business professionals. A terrible company will select a terrible hotel for you to stay in.

Why do I give all these warnings? As an expat you will often have **no idea** about the reputation of companies you interview with. If you know no one in the country you may move to, it is important to gather as much information as possible about the company before you take a job there. There is nothing worse than working in a foreign country for a foreign firm that treats its employees badly.

Remember, as an expat you typically will have **fewer** rights than a citizen of that country. That means you can be fired **at will**, can be made to work terribly long hours, and possibly have your passport confiscated legally, making your ability to flee your job and the country extremely difficult. In many countries that cater to expats, it is not uncommon for an expat, even a western expat, to be locked into a terrible job and be given terrible hours in exchange for poor pay. Workers' rights are new to much of the world, and for the most part ignored, particularly in developing countries.

My advice for anyone interviewing is the same: **act like you want to be there.** Whether by phone or in person, an interview requires the interviewee to act immensely enthused at the process. If the interview is in person, make eye contact as often as possible. Smile frequently but not enough to make the interviewer believe he or she is missing out on a joke. Never, ever, cross your arms or frown. Always keep your arms apart to make the interviewer, who may be as nervous as you, feel that you are accepting of him. Closed arms and a frown give off a sense of negativity and hostility.

I know that giving advice for properly interacting in a social situation like an interview to people who may undergo interviews in many different cultures is almost ridiculous. But I believe that to some extent showing enthusiasm and optimism for a position is a universal gesture, and I have interviewed many times in a variety of different cultures. Of course it might be that such happy and optimistic behavior is expected of Americans (my nationality) and I played right into the stereotype.

It also goes without saying that all in person interviews require the interviewee (you) to dress as impeccably as possible. Different cultures measure a person to varying degrees based on their fashion tastes, but I have yet to meet a culture that did not take the neatness of a person's dress into account. I strongly feel that a slob is less likely to be hired than someone who has taken the time to dress well. On the other end of the spectrum is someone who dresses **too well** and intimidates the interviewer. But I think this is rare.

Another issue with interviews is the difficulty in finding the time to actually fly a long distance to conduct an interview. If you are unemployed the scheduling difficulties are minimal. But if you are employed, finding the time to interview in another country can be exceptionally difficult. Take this factor into account when seeking work overseas. You may have to take a short leave of absence when applying for jobs overseas. Negotiate with prospective employers and be **candid** about the fact that it is difficult for you to travel. However, if a foreign employer wants you to work for his company, he will make arrangements and be open to your scheduling difficulties.

The best careers for moving abroad

This sub-chapter is probably the deal breaker for most readers of this book who are thinking of moving abroad for work. The truth is, it is very difficult to move abroad in some career fields. Some career fields will only allow you to move to certain countries, and other career fields will allow you to move to any country, but for terrible pay.

The Financial Guide to Working Overseas

One of the biggest misconceptions about being an expat is the idea that if you work in a medical field, you can work anywhere and be paid well. **The exact opposite is true**. In most of the world the pay for doctors and nurses is terrible. Only in the developed world are medical staff, particularly nurses, paid well. In the developing world they are paid deplorably, which is why there is generally a staff shortage issue in those countries. The developed world takes full advantage of this situation by having a huge percentage of their medical staff come from the developing world.

So if you are a doctor or nurse thinking of moving to an exotic locale for an increase in pay, **forget it**. The only reasonable move medical staff may make is from one developed country to another. It goes without saying that medical staff tend to be the highest paid in the United States due to that country's expensive private healthcare system. Whether that will continue after the inception of universal healthcare in 2014 remains to be seen.

If you wish to work in the most exotic or undeveloped locations, the jobs that are typically available to westerners are jobs in the field of **engineering** (particularly engineers involved in the mining of natural resources or the building of large government funded projects), and as staff for NGOs that assist in development. A developing country will lack the multitude of careers available in a wealthier country. There's little need for lawyers in rural Africa. From an economic standpoint poor countries interaction with world markets tends to be through **mineral exploitation** and foreign aid. The West rarely invests in poor foreign countries except in these areas, and so western employees are rarely found outside these fields.

Your Career Abroad

If you work in an office rather than **outside** your choice of overseas locations is much smaller, but **growing**, as the world continues to develop and urbanize. However, the less specialized your background, the more competition you will have with **cheap labor** from other developing countries such as India and China. If you are a computer programmer, make sure that your specialty is one not easily found in the developing world.

Expat jobs are found in countries that have a need for **people who can do things their own citizens cannot do** (or think they cannot do). The Persian Gulf is the best example of this. The oil rich countries that make up the Gulf Cooperative Council (GCC) are Saudi Arabia, Kuwait, Bahrain, Oman, UAE and Qatar. All of them have huge percentages of their populations made up of expat workers, and they remain some of the leading countries for expat careers. These oil rich countries have outsourced virtually all private sector employment and expats have benefited.

Booming industries are another huge source of expat jobs. The information technology industries as well as the medical sector are renowned for the recruitment of foreign labor. In parts of the world where mining of any kind of commodity is taking place, you can expect there to be many jobs for expats. Canada, the Middle East, Papua New Guinea, Venezuela, Nigeria and Australia, all have large mining operations and many jobs. However, as the commodity being mined is exhausted, you can expect the jobs to **dwindle** over time.

Age limitations and working overseas

Sadly, in many countries there is an age limit to being allowed to work overseas. Virtually all countries see older people as a potential burden on their healthcare systems. A working expat will most likely qualify for government sponsored healthcare as a legal worker, and obviously older people tend to have more health problems than younger people. For this reason, many countries either do not allow older expats to be given work permits (usually over the age of 60), or make it more difficult for an older worker to qualify by reducing the number of points they may be granted on an application.

However, there are **exceptions.** When I worked in Dubai, it was clearly stated that work permits were not to be granted to those over 60 except in special circumstances. The CEO of Emirates, Dubai's government owned airline was well over 70 and was of Irish background. Clearly, if a government deems you to be a valuable resource, the rule will be thrown out the window.

Age discrimination can also work against an expat as he or she **ages** in a job. A company might use an expat's reaching a certain age as grounds to have him or her removed. As an expat, you'll have to be cognizant of your new country's rules on work visa renewal and how some countries won't renew a work permit if the candidate is over a certain age. At that point you may be forced to return home.

Teaching English overseas

I am assuming that if you are reading this book, you speak English and write it well. By far the most common job for western expats overseas is **teaching English.** There are literally thousands of jobs available for someone who speaks English fluently because knowledge of English is seen as essential to conducting any international business.

These jobs tend to be given only to people from countries where English is the native language. In other words these jobs are open only to Americans, British, Irish, Canadians, South Africans, Australians and Kiwis. Other nationalities will find it difficult to get these jobs. The jobs are extraordinarily popular with recent university graduates and the schools tend to look for people with degrees.

In the European Union these jobs are really only open to British and Irish citizens. These jobs are not the highest paying, and thus it is hard to get a work permit for them. Europeans are also looking to be taught British style English, and do not want to learn the American style language differences.

One of the largest markets for English language teachers is **China.** There are hundreds of private companies hiring thousands of native English speakers to work in the schools in order to teach Chinese business people the basics of the English language. These schools are actively recruiting, and the schools are by far the easiest way for someone to get a work permit to live and work in China.

Asia remains the world leader in opportunities for English language teachers. As countries develop, there tends to be a move towards making as many of their population as possible bilingual in English. Knowledge of English is seen in many parts of the world as evidence of a person's good education and high social status.

The Financial Guide to Working Overseas

You will notice that these jobs are not really open to people from countries where English is widely spoken, but is not really the native language. Citizens of South Asian countries such as India and Pakistan will have a hard time getting English teaching jobs.

And what about the pay? Is it high? My brother taught English in China for several years and felt he was paid at the same rate as a mid-level Chinese executive, around 25-35k dollars per year. Now while this may not seem like much, with China's low cost of living this salary was very high. In more developed Asian countries with many English teaching opportunities like South Korea and Japan, pay will be considerably higher, but because those countries have high costs of living, you will not be able to live as lavishly.

Teaching English is not seen as a career by most who do it. This is in part due to the low pay (relative to their home countries), and the fact that there is little in the way of career progression for most positions. However, there are people who do make careers out of teaching English, and these people tend to become administrators of the larger schools.

The largest English language schools do not teach children but teach **adults** and it is in adult education where the highest paid jobs are. In other parts of the world there is less of a demand for English teachers, or the teaching positions are poorly paid. Latin America, for instance, does not have many lucrative positions for English teachers, nor does Africa. The only realistic places to make a career of teaching English are East Asia and Europe.

Teaching in general

The market for English teachers is large, but there are other, usually even higher paid positions for teachers who have made teaching their career and specialize in a certain curriculum or subject matter. Any country with private schools will always have a demand for foreign teachers, particularly in the developing world. Expats working in other fields who have children will always want to have their children taught to the same standard they had back home. A teacher who has the necessary credentials and some experience can easily find work abroad.

At the university level though, things get complicated. There is an enormous bias in the West **against** universities in the developing world. Someone who is making a career in higher education might be negatively affected if they seek to make their career in the universities of the developing world. The research conducted by universities in poorer countries is frequently not cited by other universities, and there is less funding to accomplish that research.

Are universities in wealthy countries better than the ones in poorer countries? According to many, yes. They have access to more resources, and research done in them is taken more seriously. If you look at any prominent western university, you will see many students and professors who have immigrated to take advantage of it for their education and careers. You do not see a similar outflow of westerners to the universities of the developing world. In fact, according to the 2009 **Academic Ranking of World Universities (ARWA)** conducted annually by a Chinese institution, Shanghai Jingtao University, all of the top thirty universities were located in Japan and the West, primarily in the United

States. For a developing world university to make this finding says volumes.

However, there are plenty of jobs for western educators in the universities of the developing world. The incentives to working at these universities are a quicker tenure track, higher pay, and more responsibilities. The drawbacks are that your work may not be taken as seriously internationally and that you will again have access to fewer resources.

Working for a Non-government Organization (NGO)

One of the more significant sources of work for expats is the NGOs. These organizations typically are "do-gooders", that is they exist in order to improve the standard of living of the countries where they operate. However, some NGOs may be based in a country simply because it is the location of their headquarters and they were founded there, like **Greenpeace** is in Amsterdam and **Amnesty International** in London.

In my experience these organizations are mainly staffed by expats, particularly from Western Europe. The pay is lower than in comparable positions in the private sector and to some extent the public sector. Obviously people who work for these organizations are not working for the money. They are working for them to make a positive impact.

It is beyond the scope of this book to criticize the effectiveness of these organizations. However, all organizations, even ones that are not profit driven **still need to make a profit to survive**. All successful NGOs allocate significant resources to convincing people, companies and governments to fund them. Many of the positions in NGOs would fall into the category of "sales" in a comparable private sector operation.

Your Career Abroad

Why is this significant? It can be an issue for young, idealistic people who go to work for NGOs and expect to simply be moved to another country in order to help others and do not realize that much of their job is to secure funding. No organization, save a government one, can exist in debt indefinitely. There are budgets that need to be maintained. This is the only reason for my warning to a prospective employee of an NGO. I personally believe that NGOs play a significant role in improving the lives of people throughout the world, and I think they remain an important career option for thousands.

As this book discusses primarily the financial aspects of life overseas, I will again state that a career in an NGO may not be lucrative, and may be more similar to life in a corporation than one would like. The structure of an NGO will have director positions and executive classes like any other large company. There will be an emphasis on budgets and debts. Most work will take place in an office rather than in the field for most people. At the end of the day you are still an employee.

In what areas do NGOs work? The number of areas NGOs work in is too large to be discussed here in great detail. Typically they could be classified as **charitable organizations.** That is they help the people of poorer countries in the areas of obtaining food and clothing, improving their environment, and gaining access to education. Many of these types of organizations are world-renowned such as the **International Red Cross** and **Amnesty International.**

I will state that NGOs and their staff tend to be internationally minded and politically left of center. That is not an indictment of their beliefs, simply a fact. In my experience people who are internationally minded and more centrist or rightist in their beliefs are drawn to work in the private sector, while those to the left of the political spectrum are drawn to NGOs and the public sector. Any organization has an intrinsic culture and you should know before you apply which culture you would be more comfortable with. Greenpeace is not looking to hire people with hedge fund experience.

There are NGOs that are backed by governments like the United States and so large that they act almost like government entities themselves. The **World Bank**, the **International Monetary Fund** (IMF), the **World Trade Organization** (WTO), and the **World Health Organization** (WHO) all wield immense power and prestige. Their criticisms and their analysis of world issues in the areas of economics and in the case of the WHO, health, are taken extremely seriously. Obviously organizations of such high regard are difficult to find employment with. An applicant should have advanced degrees from some of the world's leading universities and will face global competition for positions. Thorough knowledge of the English language is essential as most business by these entities is conducted in it.

Other large employers for expats are organizations that deal with international development. I feel that these organizations are a subset of NGOs but they make up such a significant percentage of the all NGOs that they deserve a separate but brief discussion.

International development organizations are structured in much the same way as any NGO. They spend a great deal of their time raising money, they have a managerial/corporate structure, they hire many expats. But they are largely concerned with donating food, clothing, and money to the developing world. The Catholic Church runs several large international development organizations for instance. **Oxfam** is probably one of the most prominent examples of an international development organization. This British institution donates millions of dollars every year to feeding the hungry all over the world.

Other significant areas where NGOs play a role are in the **environment** (Greenpeace, mentioned earlier is prominent in this arena), and National Geographic. Again the same issues that apply to all NGOs will apply to environmental NGOs even more so. You will work with people on the left side of the political spectrum and your idealism may be challenged as you find yourself primarily involved in a fund raising effort. These organizations are both highly esteemed in some circles and despised in others.

Foundations are typically organizations that serve similar purposes to NGOs, and in many cases have similar legal structures, but are usually linked with a company or a wealthy individual. **The Bill and Melinda Gates Foundation,** started by the wealth of Bill Gates, and when he dies, Warren Buffett, is probably the most prominent foundation in the world. Private companies can create semi-independent foundations to help in charitable areas; one prominent example is the **Ford Foundation,** which was founded by Henry Ford, the creator of the Ford Motor Company.

The legal structure of foundations, NGOs and other **non-profit** organizations requires them to put a certain amount of their revenues towards maintaining the organization and towards the organization's central activity. The term non-profit is a misnomer because all of these organizations must make a profit or risk insolvency. But that profit must be distributed to certain areas or the organization will be taxed like any other business at a higher rate. The laws governing the organizational structure of NGOs and their ilk differ from country to country, but in general are largely similar in this regard.

That structure has the consequence of depressing salaries of the NGOs executives considerably. Someone who wishes to make a career in the NGO field will find that even at the top echelons of the organization the salary, but not the responsibility, is far less than in a comparable position in the private sector.

The United Nations, the OAS and other regional government bodies

The United Nations is a quasi-government that often acts like an NGO. It has offices in virtually every country in the world, and some of the organizations within it act as giant NGOs in and of themselves. Organizations within the UN such as **United Nations Children's Fund (UNICEF), United Nations Development Program** (UNDP), **United Nations High Commissioner for Refugees** (UNHCR), **United Nations Educational, Scientific and Cultural Organization** (UNESCO) are world famous and are extraordinarily influential.

Other organizations such as the **Organization of American States** (OAS) and the **Organization for Security and Cooperation in Europe** (OSCE) behave similarly to the UN in that they publish materials that analyze various world issues and publicize efforts to improve the lives of the people of the regions they represent. These organizations are in a sense quasi-governments themselves, but because of the fact that they do not have militaries or real embassies, they lack the power to make unilateral decisions that a government can make. They are also funded by their member states, and thus are restricted in their ability to make **too harsh** statements or criticisms. Unlike an NGO which only has to answer to its donors who largely agree with the NGOs policies, these quasi government organizations have donors who wield tremendous power over them. Such a limitation can greatly limit their effectiveness and may disillusion a person who works for them.

To attain employment in the UN or any of its organizations requires a strong education and potentially knowledge of several languages. Work in these types of organizations requires an international background: this may mean degrees in international relations or in economics with an emphasis on international issues for instance. Due to the prominence and prestige of these organizations, it can be expected that attaining employment in these organizations will be difficult.

Journalism

Traditionally, journalism has always been a reliable source of employment for expats, albeit in somewhat low paying jobs. Large press organizations like **Reuters, the Associated Press, Agence France Presse** still have bureaus all over the world and have staffs of thousands. But times are changing fast, particularly in the United States and Western Europe.

One of the biggest changes in the world of the media has been the World Wide Web. Today almost every newspaper in the world is available online for free, and print newspapers have seen their subscriptions drop noticeably because online versions are available at no cost to consumers. Classified sections, another huge source of revenue for newspapers and magazines have also been taken over online by other providers.

Newspapers have cut staff, cut coverage and cut the very size of the products they produce. That has meant fewer jobs all around. Press organizations that get stories and sell them to papers around the world, like the Associated Press, have had to reduce their own staffs because the newspapers they sell to have shrunk. It is a bad time to be a journalist.

In parts of the world where online newspapers have not caught on as much yet because of poor internet infrastructure there are still many print possibilities. But the day is coming when online newspapers will completely replace print copies, and such jobs overseas are probably temporary at best. The shockwaves of the internet's effect on the world media are continuing to be felt.

Your C.V. (resume)

Most of the world writes English in the British style, rather than the American. While the United States has considerably more power and influence than Great Britain, as a legacy of the British Empire and that country's once immense political influence, British English is the norm.

For that reason, a person's curriculum vitae, or CV, should generally be written in the British format, rather than the American format. And all correspondence should be in British English rather than American English if the job you are applying for will have you speaking English regularly. A native English speaker will probably be sending a CV (don't say the American form: resume) to a company executive who is British, and an American formatted document will not receive the same attention, and may very well be confusing to the recipient!

Below is an example of a British style CV using my credentials:

RICK TODD

rick@expatinvesting.org
+44-2033938057
28A Lampard Grove
London N16 6XB

SUMMARY:

Law school graduate offers wide-ranging and multi-faceted, international financial PR expertise that would add significant value to a professional marketing environment.

EXPERIENCE:

HILL & KNOWLTON PUBLIC RELATIONS Manama, Bahrain

Senior Account Manager

2008-2009

Managed the financial clients for Hill & Knowlton's Bahrain office. Responsible for managing the largest financial clients of this dynamic business center of the region. Clients included the Central Bank of Bahrain, Gulf Finance House, Investcorp, and Capivest.

Led teams of individuals to deliver first class global public relations services to regional financial powerhouses. Oversaw media relations, client relations and all English language written materials, as well as events, press conferences and media interviews.

The Financial Guide to Working Overseas

BURSON-MARSTELLER PUBLIC RELATIONS (ASDA'A) Dubai, UAE

Account Manager, Financial Practice

2007-2008

Served as an account manager for Burson-Marsteller Public Relations' Middle East subsidiary Asda'a. Responsible in the company's financial practice for the public relations of many of the Middle East's leading financial institutions, including regional offices of large multinational banking and asset/wealth management institutions. Clients included the Swiss private bank Mirabaud, Dubai International Financial Centre, Dubai Financial Market, Dubai Islamic Bank – one of the world's oldest and largest Islamic banks – and Abraaj Capital, the Middle East's largest private equity firm.

Handled promotion in the media of IPOs and initial listings, including the IPO for Air Arabia, the first and largest low-cost carrier in the Middle East and North Africa. Also did the same for many types of mergers and acquisitions.

MANNING SELVAGE & LEE (LEO BURNETT GROUP), Dubai, UAE

English Editor and Account Executive

2006-2007

Responsible for the corporate and public relations communications of the two companies under the Leo Burnett/Publicis Group MENA. Drafted corporate communiqués including speeches for executives of the company and its clients including Nokia, Philips, Procter & Gamble, Booz Allen Hamilton, CNN, and Welcare World Health Systems.

Edited and drafted virtually all of the English language press releases of MS&L, Leo Burnett, and its clients. Wrote extensive corporate and advertising copy, including brochures, advertisements and by-lined articles on many different types of subject matter. Wrote articles and press releases on complex scientific and statistical topics for the Booz Allen Hamilton consultancy.

PROMPT COMMUNICATIONS, London, UK

Account Executive

2005-2006

Worked for a public relations firm that specialized in the IT industry, writing copy, supervising client relations and dealing with U.K. media. Gained the necessary expertise to write and interact with the UK and US media for multinational IT firms. While at Prompt oversaw diverse IT related subjects such as telecoms and long-term tape storage, and was able to maintain and manage these disparate client accounts through successful copy writing and organized marketing strategies.

AMERICAN CIVIL LIBERTIES UNION, Los Angeles, CA
Legal Triage

2004

Dealt with cases for the organization, determined whether possible clients were strong cases for the ACLU's abilities. Gained a thorough understanding of American criminal law, personal injury law, civil rights law, and constitutional law.

LOYOLA LAW SCHOOL, Los Angeles, CA

Career Service Assistant

2002

Provided information to students about potential employers and career-services functions.   Complied information on government agencies and national universities to assist students with job searches.

JON VOIGHT PRODUCTIONS, Los Angeles, CA
Story Analyst/Intern

1999-2000

Reviewed and evaluated film scripts for this Hollywood production company and Academy Award winning actor. Prepared script summaries and written recommendations as to scripts' viability. Determined who held the rights to various story properties.

EDUCATION:

LOYOLA LAW SCHOOL, Los Angeles, California
Juris Doctor 2005

Relevant courses taken: Evidence, Contracts, European Union Law, Corporations, Law of Sales, Remedies, Criminal Procedure, Civil Procedure.

BOSTON UNIVERSITY, Boston, Massachusetts
Bachelor of Science in Film and Television, Minor in Philosophy, 2001

Honors: Dean's List

SKILLS AND INTERESTS:

Your Career Abroad

Windows and Macintosh operating systems, Microsoft Word and Excel, Lexis Nexis, and Westlaw. Interests include cars, music, film, writing, travel and sports. Have a thorough understanding of the U.S. legal system and the ability to read contracts.

I would adjust the spacing as you see fit. The point of this little exercise is not for you to get to know me better or offer me a job, but to give you an example of a CV that I've written (and used) that makes use of the British format. If you have **qualifications** pertinent to your career, make them known after your education and before your skills and interests. Qualifications unfortunately are usually country-specific, and may have less relevance abroad. Adjust spacing to make the CV as visually neat as possible. No CV should be more than three pages, as the sheer volume of CVs sent to employers makes anything longer a chore to read.

Should all CVs be written in the British format? Some countries, such as the United States and France, would probably prefer CVs to be formatted in their native styles. Do the research before submitting. Is a country well known for taking in thousands of expats for jobs in your field? Is a country known for preferring to do things its own way, and ignoring foreign styles? In a way, stereotypes of a country may reveal the proper way to correctly design a proper CV.

A CV is your education and previous jobs writ large. Don't be afraid to have several CVs for different company types and job sectors. That does not mean being dishonest and hiding parts of your background. It simply means emphasizing the parts of your background that fit in with the requirements for your work. If I were applying for a job in the Middle East, my Middle East experience would be at the top of my CV. If I were applying for a job in the United States, my experience writing books and maintaining a web page would be at the top instead.

Cover letters

In my opinion, a cover letter is a way of showing your eloquence and showing what you can **offer** a company. Ask the company what they are looking for, but in such a way as to show that you are the **exact** answer to what they are seeking.

An advertisement for a job is essentially a company asking a question. The person selected for the job is the **answer**. A cover letter represents the candidate attempting to answer the question posited by the company.

Again, if the primary language to be spoken on the job is English, write the letter and all correspondence in British English. A cover letter describes **briefly** your greatest accomplishments in your career, the most prominent positions you have held, and the most significant organizations you have worked for. And it seeks to portray you as the ideal person for the job. It should be no longer than 2/3 of a page in either A4 or 8.5x11 size depending on the part of the world you applying in.

Below is a brief example of a cover letter based on one that I have used to some success in the job hunt:

Dear XXX,

Are you looking for an individual to help your organization in marketing, investor relations or public relations? My name is Rick Todd and I have extensive experience in these areas from my time working abroad in Dubai, Bahrain and

Your Career Abroad

London for various public relations agencies. I have been fortunate to work for several of the world's largest communications agencies including Hill and Knowlton and Burson-Marsteller where I handled public and investor relations for a variety of top-tier multinational corporations.

I have worked closely with regional and global media to construct and implement marketing and communications strategies for a wide variety of corporations and government entities. I have worked on clients ranging from long term data tape storage, to cosmetics to private equity firms.

My experience has immersed me in the writing and general communications requirements of businesses and government entities that seek to have a positive impact in a market. Working abroad has allowed me to interact with the business media of an entire region and I have learned to work with the requirements of media in significantly different markets and countries. I also know what it means to work in a fast paced environment in a market undergoing sustained and rapid growth, and I am looking to work in another similar environment.

I am male, 31 years old and an American national. I believe I can add significant value to your organization. Please get in touch with me to arrange an interview.

Regards,

Rick Todd

As you can see, I try to aim the letter to as broad an audience as possible. I do this for two reasons. One, it allows me to make little to no changes for each advertisement I answer, which saves me time. Two, jobs will always ask an employee to step in and do everything possible, even things that are perhaps outside of an applicant's immediate background. By stating that you are able to help an organization in the broadest sense, you make yourself more of an **asset** than other applicants.

Remember, in any correspondence you write, **always make sure you avoid any errors**. That means typographical, grammatical or factual errors. Every step of the process in the correspondence for a job is a **test**. Any misstep, and you lose out. The worse the economic climate for jobs, the more "tests". Two candidates who are nearly identical in skills and may be judged by who has made more errors in their correspondence.

Getting rejected

The most common result of a job application is **rejection**. Oddly enough, this result is hardly ever discussed in job search literature! And yet it happens all the time to even the most qualified candidates. It is such a common occurrence that the best advice I can give for someone searching for work is to **ignore it**.

Can you use rejections to help discover if you are approaching the job search process correctly? Possibly. The problem with doing this is that it will result in your making **constant** changes to your CVs and cover letters. That takes time, and it takes valuable time away from the job search process as a whole. I suggest perfecting the materials you submit and **making them general in nature** to appeal to a wide array of employers. Before sending them off into cyberspace, tweak them ever so slightly to appeal to a specific employer if you wish. But with so many people applying for any publicly advertised job, employers are looking at documents for mere seconds, and luck will play a role in getting you hired.

If something, you won't know what beforehand, jumps out of your cover letter and CV over other applicants, you'll get called in. If it doesn't, even if you're qualified for the position, you won't be called in. Finding a job, particularly overseas, takes a herculean effort. In the giant game of chance that is the job hunt, I believe that quantity with a dollop of quality is the best course forward.

Where to find the jobs

The effort to find a job depends on a number of factors, some of which may be beyond your control. If an economy is flourishing, you can expect many jobs and fewer applicants. Companies will have a mindset that they need to take whomever they can get and will take the first qualified applicant. In a tougher job market, the tables are turned and a company will be picky. And in times of terrible economic upheaval a company many not hire anyone because they are too afraid to take anyone on and risk overspending on their dwindling budget.

Because environmental factors have so much impact on the job hunt, much of finding a job is **luck** and less is skill. But there is skill involved, and there are things an applicant can do to dramatically increase his or her chances of getting hired.

The easiest way to get hired is **to be on the inside track**. The more senior the position, generally the more likely someone has been hired because of a recommendation from inside the organization. As much as the world aspires to be a meritocracy, the inside track and networking will always play a prominent or even dominant role in the selection of candidates. The key advantage to being on the inside track for a job is to be chosen before

109

the job is open to competition. Once it's open to competition, your skills and background may not look as good to the organization as others.

When a job is open to competition that generally means it is being **advertised**. Companies will look to advertise their jobs at the most popular websites and periodicals that cover their sector, but will also contact companies that will find suitable candidates for positions. These **headhunters,** as they are popularly known typically look for executive level candidates. Job candidates should make use of them, but make sure that they do not charge money. Your job search should cost you nothing except time. Employers will pay for the services of headhunters by promising them a percentage of your pay. You will pay nothing. Anyone who offers you service to find a job is probably a con artist, and should be avoided.

How do you know if the job board websites you are looking at are listing the best jobs in your field? While I cannot possibly list all the relevant job boards sites for every field of work, a good rule of thumb is that **if the biggest and most prominent companies in your field are listing jobs on the job boards and publications you frequent, you are on the right track.** If you don't see them listing jobs after a period of several days or weeks, look elsewhere.

Getting hired

If selected, you can expect to make arrangements to move to your new country, but your visa process will largely be handled by the company that picked you (if you are to work under a work permit visa). This may entail sending your passport to your employer before you board a flight, or you may enter a country on a tourist visa just like everyone else. It will vary depending on the visa requirements of the country you are to work in.

At some point in the arrival process you will have to give away your passport either to your employer or to the local government. The reason for this is that a work permit must be stamped into your passport. Make sure you have pages free in your passport, and that your passport won't expire for at least six more months. The work permit stamp is either a rubber stamp or an elaborate pasted in stamp. The wealthier the country, the more elaborate the stamp. It may take several weeks for everything to be processed.

Many countries require you to undergo some medical testing before you can officially start work. This usually means an X-ray for tuberculosis and possibly blood drawn to test for HIV/AIDS. If you test positive for these diseases, you will probably be deported and unable to start work.

You may have been told at one point to not give up your passport to an employer. Unfortunately, you will have to turn it over to your employer at some point to get a work permit. There's no choice in the matter. If your passport is lost, contact your nearest consulate or embassy. Comfort yourself with the knowledge that passports are lost daily by travelers overseas so the loss of a passport is not the end of the world. So long as you have color copies of the passport and the identification pages you should be fine.

Once your medical testing is complete, and your passport has been stamped, you'll be ready to go! Of course your employer will have had you start work before all this, but it's just an oversight. Expect the process to go smoothly. Most employers will have checked beforehand if you have anything in your background that will prevent you from getting hired. Of course, the poorer the company and the poorer the country you are going to work in, the more likely there will be oversights and less scrutiny into your background. In which case, you may get in trouble in the visa procedures with the local government.

The experience of working abroad

Nothing can truly prepare you for the experience of working with a foreign culture. In addition to the obvious difficulties such as language barriers and learning to cope with a different work culture, you will have to deal with the traditional issues that everyone encounters in a new job. This makes it all very difficult to fit in and flourish.

How can you prepare for the culture shock? My advice is to garner any cultural knowledge possible before making a move. Research by reading (if it is in a language you understand) periodicals from the region. Read books on the history of the country. Write expat bloggers living there for advice on lifestyle and how to settle in. My experience writing bloggers living in Dubai and Bahrain helped me get accustomed to life in those countries very quickly.

But in the end nothing will completely prepare you for the change. You will have to adjust or else go home. But in my experience most expats, despite their griping, adjust well. When I lived in the Middle East, I hid in the office kitchen next to the water cooler and quickly ate my lunch during the fasting period of Ramadan so as not to offend my Muslim co-workers. No one told me I would have to do that. Spending a month hiding from others to eat lunch was a culture shock, but I adjusted. You will too.

Getting fired

The longer you work overseas, the more likely you will at some point be fired from your job. Almost everyone is fired at some point in their careers, and getting fired overseas is probably a more likely outcome than if you were to work in your home country due to the lax regulations overseeing expat workers. The employees that are easiest to fire are usually the first fired.

This is the key problem with being an expat. Much of time your residency status is **tied to your job**. This means that it is quite possible that once you lose your job, you will be forced to leave the country in a short period of time. Having a western passport may minimize the risk of being forced out of the country because you may be able to switch to a tourist visa. But even on a tourist visa, you cannot live in many countries indefinitely, and you certainly cannot work legally.

And what if you have to return home? When expats working overseas are fired, many who return home assume they are eligible for **unemployment benefits**. Many countries, including the United States, do not pay unemployment benefits to their citizens who have been fired from a job abroad. Make sure you find out whether the country you are from allows you to receive unemployment benefits if you are forced to move back home.

Getting fired from a job overseas is certainly a jarring experience. You may have lost your legal right to stay in the country, and you may feel as if your rights have suddenly become truncated. If you have a family particularly children in the middle of school the moving process can be a struggle. If you are forced to leave a company, see if you can negotiate a settlement with your employer that not only pays you part of your salary, but keeps your visa going for a period of time to allow your children to finish out the school year, or at least to give you time to find another job. A good employer will make the effort, a poor employer will not. As a last resort, offer to pay your visa fees yourself, though be warned, they may cost several thousand dollars or more.

Chapter Four – Visas

Where can you work? There is almost no limit to the places you can work abroad. Before the fall of the Iron Curtain, expats were not allowed into most, if not all, communist countries except on diplomatic missions. Now, with the exception of all but the poorest and most despotic of regimes, there is no limit to where an expat can find work.

The work visa

This is granted by the company you work for. Typically you'll enter on a tourist visa, interview with the company, and then leave back to your home country. If hired, your company will arrange a work visa for you. Depending on the country, they may ask for you to send them your passport, or they may simply ask that you fly in on a tourist visa and then give them your passport. Either way, your passport will be passed on to the relevant immigration authorities.

The immigration authorities will hold onto your passport, do a criminal background check on you, and then stamp your passport with the permit. Work permits tend to be larger than tourist visas, and so the stamp will probably take up an entire page of your passport. Make sure your passport is still valid for at least six more months if not longer. Also make sure you have blank pages available.

The work visa process is pretty straightforward. You only have to pass your interview and be hired. Obviously if you are hiding the fact that you have a criminal record or have some **communicable disease** (tuberculosis, AIDS, etc.) you will probably be rejected. As noted in the previous chapter, many countries, particularly those in the developing world require you to submit to a medical examination soon after getting your work permit. They may take a blood sample to see if you are HIV positive, and an X-ray of your lungs to see if you have tuberculosis. I have had both done. More liberal western countries are usually only concerned with your criminal past (if you have one), and have laws guaranteeing the right to travel to those who are ill.

The work permit is the most popular way to become an expat. Many conservative countries only allow foreigners to live indefinitely within their country through a work permit or through marriage. However, a work permit has many potential problems for the holder.

If you are living in a country on a work permit **you are essentially an indentured servant**. What does that mean? You are only legally in the

Visas

country so long as your employer allows. If you are fired, you will most likely have to leave the country immediately or in a very short period of time. This situation can be extremely stressful and may force you to pack up your belongings and leave the friends you have made behind at a moment's notice. I've been in this situation, and it is horrible.

If you are living in a country that does not offer permanent residency to expats, I would advise you to look at your stay as a **temporary one**. This may be hard, if not impossible to do. In the Persian Gulf where there are millions of expats who will never be offered permanent residency because of government laws and traditions, many expats spend their lives growing up there and don't know any other place as home.

Parents who are planning to raise their children in this type of country should think carefully before doing so. Your child may not be able to get a job in the country once he or she graduates from school. It is very difficult for someone to start their career as an expat. Employers who are looking to hire expats are looking for candidates with several years experience. A child who grew up in an expat environment may have very little in common with his home country and will be looking to stay near his parents for a number of years.

I suggest making every effort to regularly visit your home country, and trying to establish ties between it and your child. As an expat you should avoid severing ties completely with your home. Keep in touch with relatives and friends so that your children have a community to be a part of when they leave school for their career.

Skilled migrant

There is another form of visa that is offered primarily in western countries (though the United States is a notable exception). This visa has variety of names, but essentially it allows the visa holder to work for a period of time in any job he or she can get hired at. I acquired the United Kingdom's Tier One visa in 2009 after applying (I am an American citizen). The Tier One visa is the UK's version of the skilled migrant visa.

I highly recommend this type of visa over a work permit for several reasons. For one, it allows you to have much more **bargaining power** with prospective employers. Since you have almost all the rights of a regular citizen, you can apply for any job you like (except local government jobs, as those are generally only offered to citizens), and you can leave a job whenever you like as well and not face the prospect of being forced to leave the country.

The other advantage of the skilled migrant visa is that in some countries you are allowed to be **self-employed**. If you have a business, you may be able to move it with you. If you work out of your home you may simply continue to do that. The Tier One visa that I got allowed me to start a business or bring over a business that I was running. It makes sense that a government would allow this, as a business means more tax revenue!

As you might imagine, a visa of this sort is not easy to acquire and comes with several restrictions. The visa **costs money to process**, usually the equivalent of several hundred dollars. You may also need to hire a local (the country you are applying to) **immigration attorney**. I hired a British solicitor for around US$900 in 2009. Combined with the expense for the visa, I paid around US$2000.

Do you need to hire an attorney? No. However, an attorney will know how the system works. He will be able to make sure your application contains all the correct information and is easy to understand and process by the immigration bureaucrat who handles it. Many applicants do not hire an attorney and do the process themselves and are successful. I felt my attorney gave me good advice and made the process go smoothly. I may have been lucky; I can't know for sure.

If you think about it, if you were to work as an expat under a work permit, your application would undoubtedly be handled by your company's attorneys. While the application process to work in another country doesn't usually involve a courtroom, it does involve knowing the intricacies of a bureaucracy. An attorney can help navigate those waters.

These types of visas may require periodic **renewal**. The renewal process will usually mean filling out another application, paying another fee, and supplying background paperwork to prove you have been earning the required amount of income to stay in the country. Countries that offer the skilled migrant type visa want to make sure that you are actually still a skilled migrant contributing to the economy. They don't want someone skilled moving into a less challenging career where they would compete against their own citizens. They also want to make sure that this type of migrant is not incompetent and is capable of actually maintaining his or her career while living there. The renewal process will probably not be as challenging as the initial application however.

Limitations of the skilled migrant visa

As you might imagine, there are usually limitations with any visa. Remember, you are an immigrant, and as an immigrant there are restrictions on your activities. While you have many of the same rights as a citizen, you certainly do not have all of a citizen's rights.

First, you must **qualify** for the visa. The qualifications are usually related to your **educational** background and your **income**. Countries want their skilled immigrants to actually be skilled! The universally accepted way of measuring someone's "skills" is to see how much money they make and how educated they are.

How can an immigration board determine how educated you are and how much money you've made? You will need to submit a copy of your university degrees, preferably originals or certified copies. The universities you attended will most likely have to be accredited by the most rigorous accreditation bodies in your country. That means degrees from a mail order company will probably not be accepted.

Proving how much money you've made is more straightforward. You'll need pay slips from your employer and then corresponding bank account statements. If you are self employed, bank account statements and a tax return will probably be sufficient. Check with an immigration attorney for the exact requirements.

Every country that has a skilled migrant program has a wide variety of requirements to go along with the basic ones for education and income. The income requirements may vary depending on what country you come from as well. The poorer the country you apply from, the lower the income requirement is.

There are also typically **age requirements**. Countries prefer to have their skilled migrants be as young as possible. Why? Older skilled migrants will require additional medical care (which is a burden on the government as health insurance is provided by it) and have fewer years of income tax (less tax revenue for the government) ahead of them. In applying for the UK's skilled migrant program, you actually receive more points the younger you are!

Does it all seem a bit unfair? In a sense it is. But as an immigrant you must remember that you have **fewer rights** than a citizen of that country. You don't have the right to vote. You don't (usually) have the right to join your new country's military. Whatever rights you are given as an immigrant are given as a **gift**, out of the generosity of the government. No country will give immigrants equal rights to its citizens because doing so would invite everyone in the world to move in and settle. And no country can afford to allow that many people to live within its borders.

Even after you receive your visa, there are still limitations. Often, these skilled migrant visas **expire** after a certain period. You must immigrate to the country within that period or you will lose the visa and have to apply all over again. And your visa will probably need **renewal** at least once after a period of time.

Finding an immigration attorney

In my own experience finding an immigration solicitor for the UK was remarkably easy. I went on Google, typed in "immigration solicitor" and picked one of the first companies whose website appeared. My choice for a solicitor was a good one as my application was approved, and when the UK immigration authorities sent me back my passport, they accidentally left a small note attached to it stating that my application materials were put together extremely well. It was proof that the package my solicitor had put together was well done.

I believe I was extremely lucky. The solicitor I selected had only recently started his own practice, and was young. To this day I have never met him face to face. He could have easily taken my money and never helped me. **Demand that any lawyer you might hire send you references**. Even better, find someone you know personally who has been in your situation and who can recommend to you a lawyer. Don't just click on a link, wire an individual some money and hope for the best.

Business visa

Most countries have visa programs that allow you to set up a business legally, and by doing that gain residency. I consider this type of visa to be ideal for many people because it contains many of the same benefits of the skilled migrant type visas. Also, many more countries permit this type of visa, far more than the skilled migrant visa. Even the United States has a business visa program.

There is one significant **drawback** to programs of this type. They tend to be extremely **expensive**. Countries that are looking for businesses to be set up will frequently demand that you put into a bank account the equivalent of several hundred thousand dollars or more to prove that you are serious. Other countries will demand that your business hire a certain number of local citizens. And other countries may even ask that the business be set up in a rural or impoverished part of the country. If you are wealthy and looking to set up a sham business in the urban center of a city just to get residency, think again.

Visas

However, visas of this type are essentially **giveaways** to wealthy people looking to move overseas permanently. They can afford to have a business that never makes money. Governments tend not to care so long as the business generates taxable revenue. For most people however, this type of visa is simply too expensive. The only realistic choices are a work permit, a skilled migrant type visa, or a visa through marriage.

Marriage visa

This visa is one of the most popular, and probably the visa most likely to be abused by an applicant. **Sham** marriages are commonly performed so that desperate people can gain residency into the country of their choice. Governments realize this and have taken steps whenever possible to **exhaustively** investigate marriage visa applications.

One of the benefits of a marriage visa is that it allows you to quickly move to permanent residency status. Other visa types such as skilled migrant or work permits force an individual to wait several years before he or she can qualify for permanent residency. In many countries a marriage visa **expedites** the process and lowers the number of years required before a foreign applicant is eligible for permanent residency. While the purpose behind doing this is to strengthen marriages and remove potential legal barriers for a couple, it makes this visa even more attractive to fake applicants.

Muslim countries have marriage visas, but typically only for **women**. The more conservative Muslim country will not allow a foreigner to come in and marry one of its female citizens, and even if they do, there might be severe limits on how long the male marriage visa holder is allowed into the country. The issues with marriage visas in the Muslim world are magnified when a foreign male comes from a poorer country and is trying to marry a local female. **And if you are a foreigner and of a different religion, getting a marriage visa is likely impossible**. Some of the more liberal Muslim countries (Lebanon, Bahrain) will grant a male applicant a visa if he converts to Islam. But this is very rare.

Women who have marriage visas might find that their ability to leave the country on their own will be severely restricted, particularly if they are trying to leave the country with one of their children. I've seen firsthand the issues stemming from foreigners marrying local citizens while living in the Middle East, and very frequently the foreigner's embassy became involved. On its surface a marriage visa seems like a mere formality to being allowed to live with your spouse legally. But realistically it can be fraught with difficulties.

Many countries try to investigate marriage visas by having both parties be interviewed. These interviews will assess whether the relationship of the applicants is genuine. Like many visa applications, the success of the process is up to the case officer assigned to you. In situations like this, even if the application is denied, you can be sure there would be an appeals process available.

Faking a marriage to get a marriage visa is a common practice and of course **totally illegal**. I do not recommend it under any circumstances. Perhaps the most famous recent case of a sham marriage to gain citizenship was of the redhead female Russian spy who was caught along with nine others in 2010 in the US. She held dual citizenship with the UK. and Russia and the UK citizenship was attained through an initial marriage visa. The UK promptly canceled her citizenship and banned her from the country after she was deported from the US for spying.

The consequences for lying on one of these applications are considerable. Most sham marriage visas have a foreigner quickly divorcing his or her spouse after the visa is granted. While a divorce is not in and of itself grounds for an investigation, it is bound to raise red flags. A deportation is in many cases the response of a government if they catch you in a fake marriage.

Remember also that there are often tax implications to marriage. Many countries see a marriage as one unit for tax purposes due to one spouse often not working and dependent on the other spouse's income. Take this into consideration whenever planning financially for the future of a marriage.

Refugee status

Of course another popular way of immigrating to a country is as a refugee. Typically only western democracies offer this option. I am writing this section as a little bit of a **joke**, because I know that the vast majority of refugees come from impoverished countries and are hoping to be taken into a wealthy country to avoid injury and/or death due to their behavior in their home county.

A refugee is defined as someone who cannot stay in his or her home country because to stay would mean being killed or imprisoned. That is not to say a refugee is a criminal fugitive. A refugee is facing punishment for politically speaking out against his government, for being from an oppressed minority (including in some cases for being a homosexual, which is a new trend), or for avoiding an internal conflict (such as a civil war).

Refugee status is usually granted on a case by case basis and is done through a special court system devoted to handling immigration and refugee cases. Countries usually develop these court systems specifically to handle the enormous case load of refugees. According to the United Nations Refugee Agency there are more than **nine million** refugees currently in the world.

When a country takes in a refugee they are making a **political statement**. The refuge country is essentially stating that it believes that the refugee will be **persecuted** if he or she stays in their home country, and that their belief/ethnic background is proper, while the home country's is wrong. Because western nations tend to believe alike, and developing countries tend to believe differently from western countries, the vast majority of refugees come from developing countries and move to western nations, or from one developing country to another. But hardly ever do you hear of a refugee from a western country moving to another western country.

Recently, however, in 2010 a German family **successfully** sought refugee status in the United States, causing a bit of an uproar in Germany. The family was an extremely religious Christian family that sought to home school its children. Home schooling is illegal in Germany, and the family wished to educate their children at home to give them a Christian religious themed education. Home schooling is very popular in the United States with religious parents who see the local public school system as too secular.

Visas

An American immigration court granted the German family refugee status and they have successfully moved to the United States. This is the only case I know of in recent years where refugee status was granted by a western nation to a citizen of another western nation.

That's not to say thousands of other people haven't **tried**. Hundreds of Americans serving in the military attempted to become political refugees to avoid the **Iraq war**. They typically did this by moving to Canada. During the Vietnam War thousands of Americans moved to Canada and Europe to avoid the draft, and were **accepted**. In the case of the Iraq war however, no one to my knowledge has succeeded in avoiding military service. These soldiers are not citizens avoiding a draft but volunteers breaking their contract, so their status is probably viewed very differently. Also their numbers are smaller and thus their political strength weaker.

So while it is theoretically possible to use refugee status to move permanently from one western nation to another, there is little chance you will succeed. Most western countries view themselves as fair and equitable nations giving their citizens similar rights. They don't view themselves as countries that are treating groups of their citizens poorly. For a western country to take in a refugee from another western country is to make a significant political statement that is bound to offend. For this reason it is highly unlikely we will see large numbers of refugees moving from one western country to another. But it is possible, as the Vietnam War showed. My point here is that it is not really an option for an expat.

The majority of refugees are **displaced persons** who move from a war torn country to another nearby country for safety. They tend to live in large camps and usually live in dire **poverty**. The status is not really made for middle class western expats.

Permanent residency

Many countries view legal migrants as individuals who will eventually settle in the country permanently and either become **permanent residents** or **citizens**. There are advantages and disadvantages to being given permanent residency and citizenship.

Permanent residency is usually given to a legal migrant after having legally lived in a country for a set number of years. It is almost never given automatically; you have to apply for it. This usually entails proving that you resided in the country for the required period of time. If you stayed out of the country for too long, you're disqualified and have to wait longer.

It also means proving you've never committed a crime and have been on good behavior. Countries typically want their permanent residents to be well behaved, even more so than their own citizens. That means no agitating or protesting the government. If you are seen as a troublemaker, even a legal troublemaker, you may find that your application for permanent residence is revoked.

The key advantage to getting permanent residency, in my opinion, is that you no longer have to go through the ordeal of renewing your work permit or renewing your work visa. You are no longer dependent on your employer (if residing under a work permit) to guarantee your right to stay in the country. You no longer have to pay renewal fees for your visas.

Visas

Permanent residency is the **final step** for many expats. They don't wish to get a new citizenship, and adopt the civic responsibilities that may come with that (such as jury service, mandatory voting etc.). They simply wish to legally reside in their new country indefinitely. However, when entering and exiting the country and going through passport controls, the wait may be longer and there may be more scrutiny applied to a person with permanent residency versus a person with that country's passport.

While a new citizenship will almost certainly give you additional rights (and take away some rights), you may also have additional rights as a permanent resident. Recently, there was the case of accused terrorists in the Guantanamo Bay prison who held permanent residency in the United Kingdom but were of Pakistani descent. The UK government in essence viewed them as the equivalent of citizens and pressured the US to release them.

These were individuals who had been caught fighting for the Taliban in Afghanistan. Though the exact reason for their release is unclear, it probably had to do with an agreement between the US and the UK over the UK's efforts in the wars in Iraq and Afghanistan. The prisoners were then transferred to probably far more comfortable facilities in the UK.

My point in that little example is that even without citizenship, those prisoners were given the same rights as UK citizens. Many of the advantages of holding another citizenship can be gained simply by having permanent residency in that country. However, the law is not clear in this area, and it is my understanding that UK passport holders were released from Guantanamo before permanent residents were.

As a permanent resident you may be opening yourself to additional legal liability that you wouldn't have if you were merely on a work permit or a tourist visa. You may also be opening yourself to additional tax liability. Permanent residents of the United States are treated like citizens for tax purposes and are taxed on their worldwide income. That means that if you are a foreign expat who has lived in the United States long enough to be granted a "green card" you are liable for taxes anywhere in the world like any American citizen.

Citizenship

The final step in the expat process in terms of legal settlement for many is citizenship. Generally, you can only become a citizen if you have been a **permanent resident first**. How long you must be a permanent resident before qualifying for citizenship depends on the country. You generally cannot become a citizen while on a work permit or any other kind of work related visa (like a skilled migrant visa).

Often to gain citizenship as a permanent resident you must pass a written examination. The United States is famous for this, and other nations have adopted the policy. The written examination is done to show that you know the national language and have enough of a grasp of the **local culture and history** that you will fit in as a citizen. The tests are not known for their difficulty.

After passing the exam, there is usually a ceremony where you are given a certificate of some kind and made to swear an **oath** to the country. The swearing is usually mandatory, and to avoid it will mean not being given citizenship. Every country has a natural distrust of foreigners, and though a loyalty oath in no way guarantees that a new citizen will not betray his adopted country in the future, the oath ceremony makes the new country feel more confident in its efforts to convince new citizens to be loyal.

There are many **legal repercussions** to taking citizenship. For almost everyone, a new citizenship means holding two citizenships. This is known as **dual citizenship**. Many countries do not allow this and may remove your original citizenship. Dual citizenship also means that if you commit a crime in your new country of citizenship **you cannot ask for consular assistance from your old country**. You are now a subject just like everyone else, and will have to go through the standard legal process.

Think very carefully whether dual citizenship is right for you. As a dual citizen it may become more difficult for you to travel to your home country. Many dual citizens lie to their home country and never reveal that they have two passports.

Generally, developed countries are tolerant of dual citizenship, at least for **travel purposes**. That is, you can use either passport you wish when entering an immigration check at an airport or border. It is in the developing world that it is more of an issue. Many expats choose to leave their new passport at home when traveling to their home country, or make use of their new passport for travel, particularly if their new passport gets them places more easily (has fewer visa restrictions).

There may be **tax consequences** for adopting a new citizenship. Certainly, if you gain US citizenship, you are immediately liable for taxes on any income you earn from anywhere in the world. If you move back home and your country does not have a tax treaty with the US, you may suffer double taxation.

The Financial Guide to Working Overseas

There are so many consequences to taking another citizenship that I suggest it be done only if you intend to make that new country your permanent home. It's not something to be taken lightly. With tax consequences, legal ramifications, and other potential problems resulting from dual citizenship, it may be wise to simply rely on your birth passport and permanent residency wherever you settle. But if you simply can't stand to be in the slow line at the immigration line at the airport then go for it!

Many people assume that once you have your new citizenship, you have the same exact rights as a citizen born in that country. **That is not necessarily so.** There have been several cases of people having their citizenship stripped for being convicted of crimes. In all these cases the person was an immigrant from another country who was later naturalized.

Sheikh Abu Hamza al-Masri, a UK naturalized citizen, was convicted of several counts of inciting racial hatred, soliciting murder and other crimes all related to making incendiary speeches against the UK government. For this he was sent to prison and **stripped of his citizenship**. The United States has also arrested and stripped Nazi war criminals of their citizenship before deporting them.

All of these individuals were naturalized immigrants. What I mean to show through these examples is not my love of Nazis or terrorists but that a naturalized citizen has fewer rights than someone born a citizen. If you offend your new country in some way, even if you do not **directly** commit a crime that hurts another person, you may have your passport stripped. Sheikh Hamza is not a pleasant man, but he lost his citizenship for ranting, not actually hurting anyone directly (at least that was all the UK could prove). In short, don't view a new citizenship as a get out of jail free card.

Visa run

As a citizen of a developed first world country such as the United States, UK or France etc., you will have a passport that allows you temporary entrance (usually lasting 60-90 days, perhaps longer, perhaps shorter depending on the country) into almost all of the countries of the world. In many developing countries you can actually "reside" using this type of arrangement. However, residing this way means having to take a trip out of the country for a short period of time after the expiration of your legally allotted stay. After a short time outside your new host country you then return to have your passport stamped again. This arrangement is popularly known in the expat community as the **visa run.**

When living in Dubai, I **did** visa runs a couple of times. I was between jobs and didn't have an employment visa at the time. Re-entering Dubai from a plane trip from Muscat, Oman, I came to Dubai customs and sweated out a brief wait until my passport was stamped. As I waited in line, I was sure I was to not be let back in the country or at a minimum arrested. I wasn't breaking the law, or was I? As I approached the customs agent, dressed in the traditional Gulf Arab dish-dash, I handed him my passport, and watched him gaze through it for what seemed like an eternity.

And then nothing happened. I was ushered straight through after my passport was quickly stamped. I had worried over **nothing**.

The Financial Guide to Working Overseas

My point in all of this is to tell those of you who are nervous about such things to avoid doing the visa run. I am a **cautious** type. I don't like bending the rules too much. I know I wasn't doing anything illegal due to the prestige of holding an American passport, but all the same it **felt** illegal. If I could have received some sort of permanent residency that would make me feel comfortable about going through customs, I would have applied for it. Dubai, like most developing countries or territories, frequently changes its visa laws for various reasons. Western expats in Dubai live in fear that their residency will be revoked and they will be deported. It's an uncomfortable existence.

Visa runs are also next to impossible, and most likely illegal, in the developed world. As countries become wealthier and join the pantheon of developed nations, immigrants are attracted to work in those countries. Swamped with **illegal** immigration, a country will immediately crack down and impose stricter regulation of its borders. If you decide to reside in a developing country for your retirement, and live by doing visa runs, be warned that at any moment that country's laws can change and leave you stranded. The backwater developing country you moved to might be the next developed country with very strict immigration policies. Getting permanent residency will avoid this issue.

The other reason why you should aspire to hold some sort of permanent legal residence is that it will lead to having a paperwork trail you can use to **prove** to your home country that you reside abroad and are legally avoiding **home taxation**. If you are an American citizen, and the IRS audits you, the legal document or passport stamp you have that asserts that you are domiciled abroad will come in **very handy**. Visa runs will not be seen in the same light.

You will notice that only developing countries allow them. If you must do them, be cautious. Find out from other expats if they are still allowing them. Many expats feel that in some countries, such as the Philippines or Malaysia for instance, it is too expensive to get a retirement visa, and that the visa run is a cheap alternative. You can rest assured that if the local government decides to change visa laws, the first group that will receive a **crackdown** will be the expats who commit visa runs. Don't say I didn't warn you.

Visa runs are not necessarily illegal, but if you are working and doing them, **you are working illegally.** Many countries (all poor and developing) will look the other way, but as a country becomes wealthier, and looks to make its immigration procedures stronger, visa runs are sure to go. Don't think you can make a career on a visa run. Doing visa runs should be seen as a temporary solution until you either get a new job or you move to another country. I only made use of them between jobs, and never worked while doing them. You can be sure that if you are working and doing periodic visa runs, the job you have is probably not a high paying one.

Renouncing your citizenship

Perhaps the most drastic and final act one can do as an expat is to renounce one's citizenship. The renunciation of citizenship is an uncommon act. It is usually done by those who either despise their home country, or by those who **are doing it to avoid excessive taxation**. The latter is typically the case with American citizens.

As has been mentioned before, the United States is one of the few countries in the world, and the only one in the developed world, that taxes its citizens wherever they may be. This includes citizens who live abroad. However, as of 2010, Americans are able to exclude the first US$91,400 of their income from taxation. This amount increases every year according to the rate of inflation.

According to a New York Times article from April 25, 2010, entitled "More American Expatriates Give Up Citizenship", the number of Americans renouncing their citizenship, though small has been increasing dramatically in recent years. In 2009, 743 Americans renounced their citizenship through a straightforward procedure that was conducted through their local American consulate. The article hints that the main impetus behind the increased number of renunciations comes from **strict new bank account rules** whereby American bank account holders have been unable to keep bank accounts open as their bank in the United States closed their account in order to comply with new rules from the Departments of Treasury and Homeland Security. Though the United States has no per se law against having a bank account open in a foreign country, banks err on the side of caution and will cancel your account if they feel you no longer have a valid address in the United States. The United States paranoia concerning terrorism and its obsession with destroying tax havens has made living abroad difficult.

In my time abroad, I was fortunate to have my parent's address as my permanent "home address". This stresses the importance of having someone you trust, preferably a close relative, keep an address for you open. A P.O. Box will **not cut it.**

To overcome these difficulties, some will renounce their citizenship. In general I think renouncing your citizenship is a **bad idea.** If you hold **dual**

citizenship however, it might be **more palatable.** Not having citizenship makes you **stateless** and is a very bad proposition. It means you cannot count on any government to bail you out of trouble. It means if disaster strikes, no government will make an effort to evacuate you, or compensate you in anyway. For all its flaws, and there are many, there are considerable benefits to keeping American citizenship, or any developed country's citizenship for that matter. I have also read about, but cannot confirm, that the many developed countries take a **dim view** of you when you renounce your citizenship. The film director Terry Gilliam renounced his American citizenship for British citizenship, and in order to allegedly **punish him,** he is now only allowed back into the United States for no more than 30 days a year. If this is true, it is yet another reason not renounce your citizenship.

If you choose to renounce your citizenship, I strongly recommend that your back up citizenship be from **another developed country**. The entire world is divided into a giant caste system of sorts. Citizens with passports from the United States, Canada, Western Europe and Japan, as well as a few other smaller nations, are allowed easy access to virtually all of the world's countries. Poorer countries have severely restricted entry laws. **Henley & Partners**, a global consultancy that specializes in international residence and citizenship planning publishes an annual "**Visa Restrictions Index**." This list is described as a global ranking of "countries according to travel freedom their citizens enjoy". Below is part of the 2009 edition of the list, with the number to the left of the country name signifying the ranking, and the number to the right of the country signifying the number of other countries that citizens of that named country can enter without a visa:

The Financial Guide to Working Overseas

1 Denmark 157
2 Finland 156
2 Ireland 156
2 Portugal 156
3 Belgium 155
3 Germany 155
3 Sweden 155
3 United States 155
4 Canada 154
4 Italy 154
4 Japan 154
4 Luxembourg 154
4 Netherlands 154
4 Spain 154
5 Austria 153
5 Norway 153
6 France 152
6 United Kingdom 152
7 Australia 151
8 New Zealand 150
8 Singapore 150
9 Greece 149
9 Switzerland 149
20 Argentina 127
23 Brazil 122
24 Israel 118
27 Mexico 114
35 South Africa 88
53 Russian Federation 60

Visas

61 United Arab Emirates 52
70 Saudi Arabia 42
79 China 33
88 Iraq 23
89 Afghanistan 22

As you can see from the list, poor countries, particularly those whose citizens are Muslim, have severe visa restrictions. I will also add that due to the West's reaction to the events of 9/11, citizens of Muslim countries are usually required to check in with local police whenever they visit many of the higher ranked countries on this list.

You will also notice that the countries with a considerable number of foreign retirees, such as Mexico, Argentina, Brazil and Israel, have considerably more visa restrictions than the countries of the developed world. No matter how much you fall in love with your new home, **keep your original citizenship**. You never know when you'll be planning another foreign holiday, or when you'll call upon the consular services of your home nation. There are also severe legal ramifications for having the citizenship of the country you live in as explained below.

Chapter Five – How to Invest

I believe that the primary purpose behind investing for most career oriented expats is **to save for retirement.** If you invest in order to try and get rich, the investments you make will be **correspondingly risky.** Investing should be viewed as a way of saving a percentage of your income regularly in order to fund a sensible lifestyle once you have decided to quit working later in life.

The key to successfully retiring

In general, there are two phases to saving towards your retirement. As soon as you are able to work or at least save, you are in your **accumulation phase**. When you retire, you enter your **income phase**. Accumulation is a sophisticated way of saying **saving.** That is, in order for you to successfully retire, you must save throughout your working life.

How much should you save? In general, you should save **at least 10% of your income** every year. More would be optimal. The more you save, the more likely you are able to teach yourself to live within your means and **not spend more than you make**. By far the greatest reason retirees are poor is because they neglected to save during their working lifetime. If you learn to live within your means when you are working, it will be easier to transition into a retirement lifestyle in which you can live off your savings comfortably and reliably.

When to retire

Traditionally a person retires when they are eligible for their state pension (Social Security in the United States, state pension in UK, etc.). I suggest this is probably the best time as well. For many retirees who have linked their retirement to a plan that is reliant on a portfolio of mostly equities and bonds, the **volatility** of global markets has meant that if the markets have experienced substantial losses, their retirement savings will be depleted. This problem is **magnified** when you consider that many people have made ill-advised investment decisions.

In decades past, a worker could expect to receive a small state pension that would then be supplemented by his or her company's private pension. Increasingly, companies around the world have decided that it would be cheaper to implement a scheme whereby workers control their own retirement plans. Instead of receiving a pension, workers would receive extra pay that they then could put into financial exchanges. What seemed to be a good idea at the time has been **disastrous** for many, particularly in countries like the United States and the United Kingdom.

How to Invest

For this reason, I believe that an expat who has invested poorly for whatever reason should structure his retirement so that he retires when he is eligible for his regular government pension. In fact, I would budget **my day-to-day expenses** around that pension. Such a pension is almost certainly guaranteed to be there for you. While there will always be sensationalist articles in the media about how governments won't be able to fund their citizens' retirements, I believe that governments will do all they can to do so. The most likely voters are elderly, and as a group they represent a strong voting bloc. Political leaders are loathe to offend them as a group. Even in Greece in 2010, when that country had difficulty paying government debt, the Greek leadership worked relentlessly to make sure its retirees were taken care of. Short of a complete collapse in government, I think your state pension is the **most secure** part of your portfolio. Treat it as such.

What to invest in

For most people there are really only two classes of assets to invest in. Those two classes are stocks (sometimes known as equities), and bonds (debt issued by corporations and governments). In my opinion investing in anything else is **far too risky.** That means no futures, no REITs, no hedge funds, no precious metals, etc. Historically, every other asset class has been shown to be too risky, too volatile, and delivers too little in return.

So how does one invest in these two classes? **The only reasonable way to invest in them is to use index funds**. (Index funds are sometimes known as tracker funds outside the United States). Index funds are inexpensive, typically linked to companies with high quality service, and have been shown to outperform all other types of funds and almost all individual managers over the long run.

What about actively-managed funds where a specific fund manager makes regular "picks" of assets he thinks will have the highest return? Study after academic study has shown that virtually all active fund managers are unable to accurately pick the right stocks or assets and deliver higher returns than index funds of comparable assets. What I mean by this is that an actively-managed fund of equities from the New York Stock Exchange will dramatically underperform an index fund that invests in the same exchange. **Markets are too efficient for anyone but a lucky few to be able to pick the right stocks at the right time.**

By efficient I mean that the price of an asset reacts too quickly for all but the most skilled to take advantage of it. If someone has found an underpriced stock and starts buying it up because they are convinced it will rise at some point, whatever piece of information that person had to make his decision will be known by everyone almost instantly. We live in an age of instantaneous communication. The internet, telephones, the media, etc., all have given everyone access to the same information to pick stocks. Using secret information to make stock-picking decisions is actually **illegal** and is known as insider trading. The playing field is too level.

What if I think I know someone who can pick stocks?

Chances are he has only beaten the market for a short period of time. This is a **common occurrence**. The problem is that he will almost certainly underperform the market's return (i.e. the index's return) **over time**. You must also remember that actively managed funds **are more expensive** than index funds. That means they have to dramatically outperform index funds in order to make up **for the higher fees you are paying**.

How to Invest

You might be asking at this point, What about Warren Buffett and people like him? The problem with investing with a Warren Buffett type is that you have no idea that this person is going to outperform the market **before they actually do it**. Can you time travel back to the 1950s, when Warren started investing, to take advantage of his market-beating abilities? Of course not. You can only take advantage of Warren Buffett now. As of this writing Buffett is 79 years old. There is no guarantee of how much longer he has to live. When he passes on, in all likelihood his company, Berkshire Hathaway, will be broken up. And your investment will be broken up as well. This is probably one of the best examples of the risks of **not diversifying.**

Diversify, diversify, diversify

What does it mean to diversify? Diversification means investing in several different asset classes that have little to do with each other, or at least behave **inversely** towards one another. Stocks and government bonds behave inversely towards one another in general. When stocks are up bonds go down, and vice versa. In this way, a person who invests in stocks and bonds has more diversification than a person invested solely in stocks or solely in bonds.

Index funds offer the greatest diversity, because they invest in an entire index. That means they invest in **every stock in an index** or every bond in an index. Such diversity has been shown to make for a far safer investment than investing in a small number of stocks.

Take the Dow Jones Industrial Average, an index representing American companies that are leaders in their respective industries. The companies that form the index are some of the world's largest in terms of market capitalization. When it was formed in 1896, 12 companies made up the original index. Only one, **General Electric,** is still on it. The others have either merged, or become too small to continue to be part of the index. What I mean by this example is to show you that **stock picking**, even of the world's largest and supposedly safest companies, is still risky business. If you look at the DJIA today, you will see that only seven of the 30 companies that make up the index have been there for more than 30 years. The rest have all been added in recent years.

If you think the results from buying stock of some of the world's largest companies are risky, take a look at the survival rate of smaller companies. Better to buy the entire index and have it managed **passively** for the duration of your life. You can't go wrong.

The most important rule for investing

I've discussed that the only two assets worth investing in are stocks and bonds. And I've told you that the only investment vehicles you should use to invest in those two asset classes are **index funds**. But how much money should you put in a stock index fund and how much money should you put in a bond index fund?

The general rule of thumb is **your age in bonds**. This means that if you are thirty years old, 30 per cent of your asset allocation will be in a bond index; the remaining 70 per cent will be in a stock index. **Stocks are far more volatile than bonds**. The more stocks you have, the more your portfolio will go up and down. This is why it is generally recommended that the **older you are, the more bonds you should hold**. Bonds are less likely to decline in value; however, they will never return as much money as a portfolio weighted towards stocks.

146

How to Invest

As you approach retirement, holding too many stocks can become dangerous. If your retirement is approaching in only a few years, and the market has a sudden collapse, a portfolio made up mostly of stocks could see as much as a 30-90 per cent decline. The latter actually occurred at the beginning of the Great Depression. Such a loss would be catastrophic and would take **years** to recover from.

Because bonds, particularly developed country government-issued bonds, react inversely to stocks, the more of these you hold the better you will weather any downturns in the economy. Passively-managed bond indexes, like their stock index counterparts, have also been shown to wildly outperform actively-managed funds that invest in bonds. I recommend them highly.

OK, indexes: I got it, but which ones?

Because of the importance of diversification, when it comes to stock indexes, I recommend investing only in the largest stock markets possible. If you are British, invest in the broadest FTSE index available. Americans of course, would invest in a broad index covering the various exchanges such as the New York Stock Exchange and NASDAQ together (Examples are indexes that follow the S&P 500 and the Wilshire 5000). Europeans should choose an index fund that best represents the European economy at large. Many index fund providers have European-centric index funds that comprise most if not all of the shares listed on the Frankfurt and Paris financial exchanges, giving an investor a very good representation of the European economy as a whole.

For bonds an investor should invest in a bond fund, preferably one that invests in **long term** bonds issued by their own government. If you are a

147

citizen living in the European Union, I suggest German or French government bonds. Those two countries have the most stable, strongest and fiscally responsible governments. As their bonds pay out in Euros, either is fine. Check **credit default swap** prices on each to see which the safer bet is. Germany's bonds are usually safer than French bonds by a small margin.

I am not entirely convinced that buying corporate bonds is a good idea, but buying a bond index fund that only holds corporate bonds of the **highest** credit ratings alongside **highly rated government bonds** is a good idea. Generally when stocks crash, investors quickly buy bonds, but when the stocks really crash, they tend to only buy government bonds and sell corporate bonds of all kinds. **Never buy junk bonds** or bonds with poor credit ratings, no matter what their yields may be. It's just too risky. Bonds should be viewed as a refuge from stocks, not a speculative investment.

Retirement accounts

The biggest thing to take advantage of is a retirement account. In many developed countries governments give every citizen the option of saving their money in a **tax deferred** retirement account. In the United States these are known as IRAs, Roth IRAs, 401Ks etc.; in the UK there is the ISA. These are an essential part to successfully funding a comfortable retirement. I strongly suggest you take advantage of them at the earliest possible point in your career.

But what should you put in them? The best investment vehicle to put in a retirement account is typically what is taxed the heaviest in your country. In the United States, bonds are taxed far more heavily than stocks because interest (what bonds pay) is taxed more heavily than capital gains (the profits incurred from selling a stock). Check with a reputable accountant to make sure which is ideal. In my opinion putting commodities or other items that pay no interest or dividends to an owner are not worthy of being put in a retirement account and should be held outside in a standard taxable account.

The other benefit to making use of a retirement account is that many companies that offer them to their employees also offer to match whatever amount of money you put in up to a certain percentage of your salary. **Take full advantage of this**. Matching benefits can literally double your retirement nest egg. It is literally free money.

Transferring to a better portfolio

If you decide that your portfolio is filled with too risky investments and you wish to move into more index funds or perhaps a heavier bond allocation, be aware of **tax consequences** for such a move. Typically within a retirement account there are no tax issues when selling or buying investments. But outside of one there may be very steep consequences. Check with an accountant or a lawyer specializing in taxation before making any significant changes to your portfolio.

Early retirement

Any financial discussion about retirement should at least have a brief discussion about retiring early. I define "early" as retiring before you are eligible for your state pension. I personally know of no one who has retired early and lives a normal lifestyle. Instead, the people I know who have retired early (and by retired I mean are healthy, not on some sort of disability payment) live **very frugally**.

The Financial Guide to Working Overseas

Most of the people who say they are retired early, say in their 20s or 30s are **liars.** They are selling you some sort of investment or seminar, and they describe their current lifestyle as one of luxury and opulence. In order to get your attention, they describe their life before retirement as one of overwork and despair. These people are professional con artists, and you should ignore them. They tend to appear on late night advertisements on cable channels in the United States; most European countries have banned them. You can still see their websites online, however.

If they were telling the truth, they would not be on television hawking things. That in and of itself should be a red flag because it means they are **not retired**, but actually working, in this case working to steal your money. Retiring early is possible, but it requires an enormous effort, and it requires **extreme saving and permanent frugality**.

The key to retiring early, as I see it, is to save a substantial amount of money. This will require either a **windfall** of some kind such as an inheritance, or the sale of a valuable asset such as a paid off home or a company you owned. Or it will require a **high salary**, the bulk of which is not spent but saved for a period of several years. Again, depending on the amount you have saved, in all probability you will have to live an austere existence. Why? Because retiring early means that you will live for a much longer time than the normal retiree. Most people who retire are in their 60s, and with a life expectancy in the late 70s or early 80s, only need to save up for that period. Someone who retires earlier will have to save for a much longer period of life.

Another risk to retiring early is that you will fail to make contributions to your state pension. Most state pensions are linked to income contributions made over the entire period of your career through taxation. If you retire before you are **eligible** for your pension, or before you can receive your **full** pension, you will reduce the most **guaranteed** income in your portfolio. In my opinion it is an unnecessary risk. In general, retire later than sooner.

The biggest risk of following the advice of someone who advocates retiring early is that they typically will advise the use of **leverage** to buy stocks, or to **flip property**. Both acts are very risky, and entail the use of **borrowed** money. While one action involves stocks, and the other property, because both are extremely risky, they tend to work only in strong **bull markets**. To succeed they require substantial **luck** rather than skill. I advise against either as a strategy. Historically, American stock markets decline in one out of every three years. Property market rises and falls largely coincide with the larger rises and falls of equity markets. If your leveraged investment declines in value, not only will the money you invested be gone, but you will also be indebted to the financial institution that lent you money in the first place.

The smarter strategy is **patience**. Accumulate your portfolio through the magic of **compound interest**.

Compound interest: the surest way to wealth
Allegedly Benjamin Franklin called compound interest the **eighth wonder of the world**, while Albert Einstein called it "the world's greatest discovery". Benjamin Franklin made use of compound interest by willing US$4400 to the cities of Philadelphia and Boston in 1785 to collect interest for 200 years. By 1990 more than **two million** dollars had

accumulated from this small sum in Philadelphia, and **five million** dollars from this amount in Boston.

Compound interest can work for you, and is the only surefire way to accumulate money throughout your life. If you can find a set of assets that produce income or rise in value over time, and you buy more and more of them throughout your career, through the magic of compound interest you can achieve financial independence.

The trick to making compound interest work is **saving**. If you do not consistently save throughout your life, you will be hard pressed to retire comfortably. Saving is the single biggest factor to having a successful retirement. In order to save you must live within your means, throughout your life. That means as little credit card debt as possible, and as little debt as possible **period**. Successful retirement is a state of mind, not just a mathematical construct.

A rule of thumb I use is to save **at least 10 per cent** of my income every year. Never any less than that, and often times more than that. By putting this chunk of money in relatively safe investments such as index funds, I allow my money to grow steadily over time.

Length of life

One of the key elements in planning your retirement should be an understanding of your potentially **long life**. Obviously, if you were to fall over dead tomorrow, any retirement planning you've done would be wasted. I would argue that you should plan your retirement with the belief that you might very well live well into your **nineties**.

How to Invest

Currently, all developed countries can expect their citizens to enjoy an average life expectancy of almost 78 years. In several developed countries, including Canada, France, Australia, Italy, Japan and Sweden, the average life expectancy is over the age of 80! If you slice into those statistics and view separate socio-economic classes such as females, the upper class, and the upper middle class, life expectancy rises even further. In general, **the wealthier and better educated you are, the longer you are going to live**, as you have access to a better diet, better healthcare, and a safer environment. Women, for various genetic and biological reasons, normally outlive men. Take all these factors into account when considering your lifespan.

You can also never underestimate what advances in medical technology will be available to you as you age. However, the poorer the country you immigrate to is, the less likely you will be to have access to such treatments.

My point in all this is that you should never underestimate how long you will live. Spending wisely, and living within your means should be done throughout your life, and throughout your retirement. Even if you have no plans to leave anything to your heirs, spending everything you have on a luxurious lifestyle could mean poverty in the last years of your life.

Investing for retirement is actually easy

There is a common misconception in investing. You are told by so-called financial professionals that investing is difficult and that you need a professional to help you. **The opposite is true**. Financial advisors almost always add little or no value to a portfolio. Instead, through high fees and bad advice they **subtract value**, at times dramatically so. Financial advisors wish to appear on the same levels as doctors, lawyers, engineers and accountants. They drive nice cars and live in big houses. They often have a three-letter acronym after their name like "CFA", "CFP" etc. These titles are in no way, shape or form as hard to get as MD, ESQ, or CPA, nor is oversight of financial planners as thorough as that of other professions.

You should manage your portfolio **by yourself**. In fact, **fire your financial planner** if you have one now. The only time I suggest dealing with a financial planner, if you absolutely cannot stand to look at numbers, is to use one on a **fee-only basis**. That way they have little to no control over your finances, and you can take or leave their advice.

Mutual Funds and ETFs

The best way to invest in indexes is to invest either in mutual funds or exchange traded funds (better known as ETFs). ETFs are essentially funds that are listed on a stock exchange like any other stock. You can buy them through any broker.

Mutual funds must be purchased through a mutual fund company. The largest fund companies in the world offer index funds. There's no need to be exotic in your choices; the largest companies also tend to offer the best index mutual funds.

Basically there is an ETF for every version of an index mutual fund. So which should you choose? I would suggest whichever you are more comfortable with. ETFs are usually cheaper than their respective mutual funds, but not by a great deal. If you purchase an ETF you also have to take into consideration the fees charged by brokers. These can be expensive, but there are usually plenty of options in this area so you can afford to be choosy.

The advantage of mutual funds over ETFs is that you gain access to the **support staff** of the mutual fund company. Brokers are not in the business of offering you 24 hour a day support for your account; they are in the business of buying and selling shares. The small additional expense of a mutual fund may be worth it in this regard. Many mutual fund companies now offer ETF versions of their funds as well, making the differences between both virtually moot.

I am biased in that I believe **Vanguard** to be the pre-eminent indexing mutual fund firm. I do not believe you need to make investing complex by hiring middlemen to buy funds for you or to make fund decisions for you. The beauty of the indexing approach is that you simply save money and don't worry about the ups and downs of the market. Over time, you will more than likely have accumulated considerable wealth. But you must be patient, and you must **avoid** being **tempted** into other investment vehicles.

Use a retirement calculator

How do you know when you are ready to retire? How do you know if you have saved enough for retirement? Do you know, based on how much you've saved, how much you can spend in retirement?

Google "retirement calculator" and dozens will come up. I recommend Firecalc.com. This website takes into account various changes in inflation over an almost 150-year period. It's in dollars and not other currencies, unfortunately. But the idea is a sound one: **you can calculate how much you can safely spend from your savings based on the past**

performance of stocks and bonds. However, remember that past performance is not a guarantee. The future is inherently unpredictable.

No retirement calculator will be 100% accurate. It cannot predict the future. The Euro could collapse, the dollar could collapse, anything can happen. The longer you are retired, the more vulnerable you are to significant changes in the world's economy. A calculator gives you a very basic idea as to how much you can spend comfortably without depleting your savings.

Avoid debt like the plague

As you approach retirement, or if you are in retirement, I suggest you avoid debt whenever possible. Debt comes in many forms, but perhaps the most common is credit card debt. Credit cards routinely have interest rates above 10% which compounded annually can make a debt grow spectacularly. The interest rates on some credit card debt would make a loan shark blush.

For retirees on a fixed income, credit card debt represents a significant reduction in savings. Prioritize the paring down of credit card debt over other expenditures whenever possible. It's that damaging to your bottom line.

Where to learn about investing for retirement

The best place to go for retirement investment advice regardless of where you are located or what your nationality is, is the **Bogleheads** community located at www.bogleheads.org. This group of investors comes from all walks of life and many countries throughout the world. Don't be put off by the fact that most of the people at this forum are American; there is expert advice available for all nationalities, and expats living abroad routinely ask for financial advice on where to invest and where to save their money.

The forum is named after **John Bogle,** one of the financial titans of the last forty years. John Bogle founded the **Vanguard Group**, the world's largest mutual fund company. Through his leadership, Vanguard became the first company to offer retail investors an index fund, Vanguard's **Vanguard VFINX** in 1976. The fund has gone on to become the world's largest with more than US$91.1 billion in assets under management. The fact that this fund has lasted this long, and manages this much money, is a tribute to the success of indexing and proof that this method of investing is better than any other for the average investor.

One of the mantras of the Bogleheads and many others who index invest is that a person should **avoid the noise**. That is, you should allocate money to your investments and let them do their work. Don't fall for advertisements or newspaper articles that are really advertisements in disguise, which argue that this or that investment is better and will "beat the market". Simply allocate according to your risk tolerance between equities and government backed long term bonds, and save regularly. When you retire you will have amassed a comfortable nest egg with which to live well in retirement anywhere in the world.

The Financial Guide to Working Overseas

Chapter Six – Practical Matters

Though the bulk of this book is related to moving and working abroad from a financial standpoint, I feel there is a need to discuss the small things, *the practical things*, in regards to moving overseas. Moving to another country is far more difficult and complex than simply moving to the next city over. It requires a fundamental shift in the way you think about things. Language, driving, food, clothing, all these things may be dramatically different from what you are used to. This chapter will seek to give some general advice on moving abroad from the most practical standpoint possible. Feel free to skip this chapter if you are solely concerned with the financial aspects of working abroad, however, some of the advice in this chapter will help you save considerable amounts of money.

Language

It is possible to not know the language of the country you're moving to and do fine. I don't speak Arabic and have lived and worked in two separate Arab countries. Granted, almost everyone in those countries spoke English, and in Bahrain there were thousands of my fellow Americans living on a giant naval base, but speaking the local language would have helped immensely. How? It would have **saved me money**.

The best reason I can think of for learning the local language is the day-to-day savings you will experience interacting with local merchants and businesses. For instance, taking a cab might become remarkably cheaper. If you speak the local language well enough, you'll be able to bargain for a better fare (particularly in the developing world), and you'll be seen not as a tourist but as either a local or someone who understands the intricacies of local life. Tourists get ripped off, natives don't. If you don't know the local language and are dependent on English-speaking businesses, you can expect to pay considerably more for everything.

The other big reason to learn the local language is **legal**. For every contract you sign, for every court case you're involved in, you're going to wish you spoke the local language. Contracts that are professionally drawn up always contain labyrinthine language designed to confuse the signatory and protect the contract drafter. In a court case proceedings will always be conducted in the local language, and never in yours. Knowing the local language can be the difference between jail and freedom.

That's not to say you absolutely need to learn the language. You can get by with a **pidgin** version of the local language that makes use of some local words and hand gestures. It's very easy to do this, and I've certainly done it in my travels. But more importantly you should pick up the locals' hand gestures and actions yourself. This will enable you to sense danger, and to sense if you are getting ripped off or betrayed. I view language as a sort of **awareness** of what others are doing around you. The better you understand the language, the more aware you are of others' behavior and actions.

The best way to learn a foreign language is to **immerse** yourself. That means talking to people other than your fellow English- speaking expats. It means making friends with locals, dealing with merchants on a face-to-face basis, and taking language lessons. Most countries have language immersion courses that cater to English-speaking foreigners. These typically last a week to a month and cost only a few hundred dollars per course.

Driving

One of the biggest issues in living abroad is the change in driving styles. This is particularly true when comparing the developed world with the developing world. Typically on developing world roads you will find:

- Many drivers who regularly speed at deadly rates
- Drivers who rarely or never use turn signals
- Drivers who rarely follow street signs, or obey stoplights
- Drivers who throw trash out their windows, most commonly cigarettes
- People crossing highways as they would an intersection (and regularly getting killed for it)
- Accidents, including lethal ones, a very common occurrence

Driving in the developing world takes lightning-fast reflexes, and a thorough awareness of all that is going on around you. You must be an experienced defensive driver, and you must drive aggressively or you will be run off the road. In many countries it is typical for a person speeding to tailgate your car and flash his brights, signaling you to get out of his way. There is very little concept of road manners or safety.

This is a **serious concern** to someone who is used to driving on relatively safe highways back home. While a complete overview of automotive safety is beyond the remit of this book, it is important to know some basic guidelines:

1. The **bigger** the vehicle you drive, the safer you will be. The counter to this is that in a crash the larger vehicle is more likely to kill the other participant. I am going to avoid a debate on the ethics of driving a large vehicle like an SUV or pickup, but simple physics tells us that a larger mass smashing into a smaller one is likely to do the smaller vehicle considerable damage. A bigger vehicle **driven responsibly** will cause other drivers to steer well clear of you. Another added benefit of a large vehicle with considerable ground clearance is that it will be able to traverse open ground more easily, which is a consideration when living in a poorer country.

2. Make sure the vehicle you buy has **electronic stability control (ESC)**. According the National Highway Traffic and Safety Administration, ESC reduces accidents by 35 per cent. ESC is a computer device that detects when your vehicle is about to skid, and applies the brakes in order to steer your vehicle away from a

skid. Skidding a vehicle usually means a loss of control and a possible rollover of your vehicle.

3. Watch out for animals on the road, particularly those that are being herded across by a shepherd. This is obviously far more of an issue in rural areas, but there are dozens of animals that regularly cross roads in order to graze or find water, such as sheep, camels, goats, horses, llamas etc. Smashing into them in your car will do far more damage to your vehicle than you can imagine. In addition to that, if you have killed an animal owned by someone else, you can bet that you will be liable for the animal's death and that you will face a heavy fine and a possible court appearance.

4. Obey traffic laws **but only as long as everyone else does.** It doesn't make sense to follow the speed limit in a third world country when everyone around you is speeding. Going slow when others are going fast will turn your vehicle into an **obstacle** and you will be hit from behind. This is probably contrary to almost everything you've been taught, but then again driving in a third world country is illogical and borderline insane anyway. There is a sense of fatalism in all drivers in these countries that have long since abandoned even the pretense of safe driving. When in Rome....

5. It makes more sense to obey the **laws of the jungle** when it comes to driving in a developing country. These laws include the periodic bribery of traffic cops, speeding to keep up with the traffic, driving aggressively, and ignoring street signs if obeying them would mean endangering your life.

Other guidelines that are obvious but bear repeating are that you should always wear your seatbelt, that you should always keep your eyes on the road, and that you should avoid doing anything to distract yourself. That could mean talking to a passenger, using your phone etc. While I have instructed you to copy other drivers around you, you should only copy those behaviors that will save you. You must be **a better driver** than those around you. If the people around you in traffic are chatting on their cell phones while speeding, you should speed but not chat on the phone as well. You need to be more aware than the next guy, and instead make mental notes on his stupid behavior so you prevent him from crashing into you.

My solution to the dilemma of driving abroad, particularly in a poorer country, is that you consider **hiring a permanent driver if the option is affordable**. By hiring a driver I mean hiring someone with their own vehicle, rather than hiring someone to drive yours. That means if your driver gets into an accident while driving you, since he is the owner of the car, he will probably be liable instead of you.

Every country has different cultural **idiosyncrasies** when it comes to driving, and only a native will know them all. I feel that this is such an important issue that you should put it into your **budget** before you move abroad. The most dangerous daily activity almost everyone does is to drive a car. In poorer countries, that danger is magnified dramatically. Scary statistic time: according to the WHO, traffic accidents are the leading cause of death for 10-24 year olds, and 600 people a day are killed in traffic accidents in China. I can tell you from my own experience in the Middle East that the combination of cheap oil and high-performance cars made surviving the drive to work every day unharmed a miracle.

Practical Matters

Hiring a driver has the added benefit of possibly helping you **avoid traffic.** Poor countries and countries experiencing strong economic growth (as is more typical in developing countries than developed ones) tend to have horrible traffic congestion, as road-building and public transport cannot keep up with the growing numbers of cars being put on the road. A driver will know all the various side roads and alleyways you can drive through to avoid traffic and get to your destination on time.

I am not a big believer in having the **license** of the country you are driving in. I believe an international license combined with your passport is often **good enough**. There may be considerable disagreement with me on this issue, but I feel there is a certain power and prestige to flashing your passport, particularly if it is from a wealthy country. I had to appear before a traffic cop at a police station after an accident that was largely my fault while I lived and worked in Bahrain, as was the law for any accidents that occur. I did not have a local driver's license, but I had a license from a neighboring Gulf country which was valid, and I had my own license from the United States. I also had my passport. The traffic warden found in my favor even though I had rammed the other person in the back while speeding. I believe, though I have no way to prove this, the fact that Bahrain is the home to a large US naval base and thousands of American sailors got me off. The other person's insurance had to pay for the accident. Other readers may have experiences that have led them to a different conclusion, however. Your passport, and a bribe, may be enough to get out of any accident that police are involved in.

It is for this reason that you should keep your home driver's license for as **long as possible**. I will discuss later in this book the importance of keeping a home address for billing and healthcare purposes. Keep it as well to be able to maintain your driver's license. Your license is a valid form of identity, and saves you the need for lugging your passport (a far more important document) around with you. I feel it is a get-out-of-trouble card in many countries, and it shows a police officer that you are probably a competent driver (even if you are not).

The rules are entirely different in the developed world, and of course traffic laws should be followed there. Bribing traffic police and ignoring signs should be avoided at all costs. While I understand that this part of the book is almost completely devoid of politically correct discussion, and you could argue that I am advocating breaking the law in poor countries, driving is such a dangerous and yet necessary part of life that I feel it would be irresponsible of me to write anything less than what I see as the truth, particularly when it comes to the safety of others.

If you feel you must absolutely buy a car, then **buy a car brand that is popular in the country you where you choose to live**. If you live in Mexico, you will find that while Nissan and Volkswagen are popular, Toyota is not. In the Gulf, where I resided for three years, the most popular brands were Toyota, Peugeot, and Chevrolet. Buying a brand that is uncommon or imported into the country you live in will mean **costly repairs** and **a bad or small dealer network** that will be hard to get to when you need to do repairs. The key is to find out which companies actually **build the cars in the country**. For instance, if you choose to live in a Latin American country that has a Chevrolet factory that builds a certain car, buy that **exact car.** The car will be cheaper since there are no tariffs on it, and replacement parts will probably be cheaper as they will most likely be built locally too. The car will be popular because of its low cost, making repairs cheaper and better, as mechanics will have more experience repairing the car.

When I was living in Dubai, to save money I bought an Opel Astra in Sharjah, the neighboring Emirate. The problem with the car was that it was an **unpopular** vehicle for the region. It was small, and a hatchback. In a country where the price of gasoline is little more than a dollar a gallon, people want big cars and big SUVs. I was forced to sell the car at a loss (relative to what I owed on the vehicle) when I had to move to another country for work and ended up selling it to an Azerbaijani used car trader who specialized in taking unwanted vehicles to his native country and re-selling them on the grey market there. He made a hefty profit on my low mileage car, and I did not. If my car had been more popular, I would not have had to deal with this issue.

I also suggest that you **do not import a car** on your own. The costs associated with this are usually high. Not only do you have to pay shipping expenses including insurance, you also have to pay import tariffs. In many developed countries, importing cars yourself is next to impossible due to safety restrictions. Developing countries may see an imported car as a vehicle that competes with vehicles built by their own factories and will tax it heavily. **Buy locally**.

Finally, if you must buy a car for whatever reason, make sure to buy one that is **cheap,** because of the effects of bad roads on your vehicle (less of an issue in the developed world). The nicer the car, the more horrified you will be when you see the scrapes caused by road pebbles tearing tiny chunks out of your new paint. Always remember that a car is yet another asset that can be broken into or stolen, and the nicer the car is, the juicier the target it makes for potential thieves.

In regards to **auto insurance**, I believe you should always have it, even if owning it is not enforced in the country you live in. It is in the poorest countries that the traffic accident rates are highest, and if you live in a poor country, you will at some point be involved in an auto accident. Insurance brings peace of mind, but more importantly, it will lower repair costs for a car that has been damaged in the all-too-regular occurrence of traffic accidents. In some countries, like Mexico, if you are involved in a traffic accident without insurance, regardless of who is at fault, you can be held by the police without trial until fault is determined.

Television

For many who move abroad, TV is the last thing on their minds. For others, like myself, being away from your favorite sports team is painful. It simply isn't the same reading scores on the internet. Local cable television and satellite are frequently **not adequate.** Their content is dependent on the company that runs them, and they are unlikely to give you the channels you want to see. If you are fan of American sports, or regionally-popular sports like cricket and rugby, you will not find your teams televised in a country that primarily plays soccer. The best solution I can think of is streaming videos on the internet. Of course the quality of these will not only depend on your computer, but **on the bandwidth access** of the country you live in. Various commercial websites have thousands of films and movies available for free but with commercials, and of course it might be possible to access your favorite sport's website for streaming video. Typically you will have to pay for those.

Practical Matters

If there are considerable numbers of your nationality, you might try the local pub or bar that caters to expats to see if they will air your favorite sport. For television and film, Hollywood fare is easily available through **illegally copied DVDs** in much of the developing world. Most EU countries will not allow you to travel back with these, and they will be confiscated. The United States is far more liberal and allows you to have one copy of each movie you have purchased but no more. If you are looking for rarer shows and films, **BitTorrent** is your friend. I won't say any more on the matter as all these tactics for acquiring media are quite unsavory.

Hygiene and sanitation

If you are new to living and traveling abroad, you might be unaware that many countries, particularly poorer ones, have issues with personal hygiene and sanitation. While there is little you can do about others' personal hygiene, except grin and bear it (and bear it you must, for you will be surprised as to how much other people can smell), there is something you can do in regards to sanitation.

One of the biggest issues with sanitation in the developing world is the continued dumping of **untreated sewage** into bodies of water that people play in. In countries that are experiencing substantial **economic growth**, infrastructure is overstretched, too many people are moving in, and sewage systems overflow. In the mind of local government, the best solution is to build a pipe from developments to the nearest body of water.

This is particularly true with **new developments**. Since developers are usually closely associated with the corrupt government, their goal is to build units first, and worry about infrastructure later. These new developments are the biggest culprits in polluting bodies of water with sewage.

The only solution I can think of is to move near a body of water that is surrounded by older developments that have been built to cater to locals, rather than expats. Either that or avoid the water as much as possible. These aren't the best choices, but in many countries where pollution is endemic, you have to make do the best you can.

The importance of the internet

Besides acting as a potential television replacement, the internet can **allow you to make cheap phone calls.** Companies like Skype allow you to use your internet connection to transmit voice data just as you would use a phone. In some countries however, companies like Skype are banned, and the monopoly phone system is the only way to make a call. To avoid this, I suggest using a **virtual private network (VPN).** A Google search for VPNs will show you hundreds of companies that will set one up for you for a small monthly fee. I used vpnaccounts.com a few years ago in order to access Skype when I lived in Dubai, where it was banned to force residents to use their expensive, monopolistic, state-run phone system. A VPN convinces your internet service that you are really accessing it from another country, and it allows you to bypass any server's restrictions. Any and all banned websites are now free to watch.

Another important aspect of the internet is it gives you the ability to **pay your bills and do banking.** If you move abroad you will have to rely on the local postal service, and it will probably be inferior to your home one. This will be particularly true if you choose to live in a rural area. I would

Practical Matters

suggest handling as much of your postal and banking needs online as possible.

If you decide to live in a rural area, particularly in the developing world, you will probably need to purchase **satellite internet**. While almost all countries have Wi-Fi access in every city center, in rural areas high speed internet access is a rarity. The problem with satellite internet is that it can be **very expensive**. I believe it is worth it, particularly if you do your banking online and make international phone calls via VoIP.

Depending on where you live in the world, you must use a particular service, as only certain satellite internet providers have satellites over given continents and areas. Satellite internet services are usually a few hundred dollars (US) per month depending on how fast a connection you wish to purchase. VoIP works well even with low speed connections, so you may be able to skimp on this expense to some extent if your sole purposes for internet access are bill-paying and phone calls. However, satellite internet requires a somewhat steep initial fee in order to be sent the necessary equipment (an actual satellite **dish**) which you will probably only lease for the duration of your contract with the company.

If you decide to live in **North or South America** the following companies offer services: Skycasters, Enterprise Satellite Solutions (ESS), and VSAT Systems. This includes the Caribbean. VSAT Systems does not cover southern Mexico. IsoTropic Systems covers almost the entire world. Bentley Walker covers only South America. Elite Satellite only covers North America and the Caribbean.

For **Europe,** the following companies offer services: Avonline, IsoTropic (though not in all of Eastern Europe), BusinessCom (only Eastern Europe and not all of Western Europe), GlobalTT, and Bentley Walker. For **Asia**, BusinessCom offers comprehensive coverage. For **Oceania**, DigitalSkys covers Australia, but not all of New Zealand.

This list of providers may not be complete but should give you a good start. In areas with more providers you should expect more competitive pricing, and in areas with fewer providers, you should expect higher costs.

Mail

Before you move, find out if the country you are moving to has a decent postal system. If it does, don't bother with using a mail forwarding system but just have everything sent to your new address. If it doesn't, you will have to either find a mail forwarding system that is reliable, or depend on someone you trust to send you your mail. You may find that relying on a close relative to take care of your mail is an incentive to communicate with that person regularly. Obviously if you have anything you are unwilling to let anyone know about coming to you in the mail, you should not do this. You could also try the company **Earth Class Mail** which will read your mail and convert it to email. They are easily found through a Google search. I have friends who have used the service, but while it is good, it is also expensive.

There is however, another incentive to keeping a home address. The United States has very strict rules for its citizens when it comes having a **foreign bank account**. Many banks, if they determine that you are living overseas and not in the United States, will cancel your account for fear of inadvertently assisting someone in hiding money in an offshore account or helping a **terrorist**. It is **not illegal** for Americans to live abroad, but it is more difficult than for citizens of other developed countries. In order for you to maintain your bank account, I suggest you maintain an address back home. I do not mean a P.O. Box. Depend on someone you trust to collect at least your bank statements. It is not the best situation, but until laws are changed to make it more amenable for Americans to live abroad, it is a situation you will have to live with.

Banking

No matter where you live, you will always need the services of a local bank branch. As with many aspects of living overseas, there is a set of rules for developed countries, and a set of rules for developing countries. When moving to a developing country, before going abroad I would find out which **banks from your home country** have established themselves in your retirement destination. If you do not have an account there, I would open one. By having a home country bank account and a retirement country bank account at the same bank, you can more easily transfer funds back and forth, avoid ATM fees, and more importantly, there is less of a possibility that **your bank will collapse.** A local bank is far more likely to collapse, and to take your money with it. Local accounts are hardly ever insured in the case of bankruptcy or insolvency. With a large bank that is based in your home country there is the possibility, **not guaranteed,** that your money will be insured by your home government even though it is abroad.

One example from history I came up with was as follows: When the communists came to power in Russia in 1917, they seized the local branch of Citibank, then called First National City Bank. The depositors who managed to get out of Russia sued Citi in the US, but the courts backed Citi, and Citi never made good on these deposits.

An alternative that I have not investigated, but have read about and think shows promise, is to open an account in your home country at a **bank or other financial institution that does not charge ATM fees**. With a card issued by this financial institution you could travel anywhere in the world, and use any ATM without hassle. However, make sure that this deal is one that is permanent. In many cases the offer is only made to attract customers, not to be a permanent part of the bank's marketing strategy. If the rules are changed when you are abroad, you'll be in trouble.

Another important factor in choosing a bank is whether you can conduct **online banking**. Make sure that the bank you choose has a reliable online setup that you are comfortable with and that will not lose your money if you make transfers and the like. Many poorer countries' banks are not online, which can lead to difficulties. Virtually every bank in the developed world is on-line, except the very smallest. Choose only those that are online for your banking needs. You will avoid a paper trail in the event of a move, and you will be able to organize yourself far more efficiently.

For this reason, you should keep **as little of your money as you can** in a developing nation. In the event of a financial collapse, hyperinflation, or some sort of government action that freezes your account, you want to lose as little as possible of your nest egg. The safest thing you can do is to leave the bulk of your hard-earned money at home where it will more than likely be safe.

Practical Matters

In Mexico in the 1970s, banks offered accounts where the deposits could be held in dollars. This was seen as a way of attracting Mexicans to make use of the banking system which was (and is) notorious for routinely collapsing. The idea was that dollar denominated deposits were actually worth something, and that deposits denominated in pesos threatened to dissipate in value in the event of hyperinflation.

However, the Mexican government saw through this stunt and dollar deposits were **force-converted** into pesos when the peso was devalued to combat hyperinflation. This action has happened recently in other countries such as Pakistan and elsewhere in recent years. The lesson is this: if it's in a foreign bank, denomination in your home currency will not be enough to save you.

When moving from one developed country to another, the safety of banks is far greater, and you probably shouldn't worry about losing your money in the event of a bank collapse. While European countries may not guarantee their depositors' accounts, the events of the recession of 2008 show that all Western European countries will do whatever it takes to prevent a **bank run** or loss of depositor confidence. It is one of the many signs that a country is developed that it can insure the protection of money invested in its local banks. The reason for that confidence is to attract future investment from abroad and from its citizens. Developing countries, sadly, are not in a position to offer such **reassurances** and you should use caution in leaving your money to their care.

In many countries it is exceptionally difficult to even open an account. Letters of reference may be required, as well as credit and background checks. In many countries it may take a considerable period of time. This is probably the most important reason for you to keep your old bank account open indefinitely. Closing your account and hoping to open a new one overseas will mean holding onto considerable sums of cash for a long period, which is always a **risky** prospect.

Offshore banking

There is another type of bank account that is relatively easier to open than a standard checking or savings account overseas. Offshore bank accounts are seen by many as an ideal way of hiding money from their home governments in order to avoid paying tax. While tempting, I believe opening these accounts is very dangerous.

Western governments, particularly those of Germany, the United Kingdom and the United States, have all made increasing efforts in recent years to crack down on their citizens who are hiding money in offshore accounts. **It is often illegal to have money stashed in offshore accounts and not report it to your government.** In the United States in particular, it is illegal. The days of the successful businessman being able to elude the tax man are coming to an end in this new era of increased government oversight of the financial sector in the wake of the recent market crash. Avoid becoming a casualty and report all income from foreign sources if you are required to do so.

Offshore banking is primarily for the very rich. They can afford to have their money earn 1% interest or less, and they can afford lawyers to defend them from tax authorities if they are accused of tax evasion. Chances are, you cannot afford to put your money in an offshore account for tax evasion purposes. Most people need to grow their savings over the course of their career so they have enough to retire.

Practical Matters

The only way to do that is to hold substantial percentages of your savings in stocks at all times. The last few years have seen dismal returns to stocks, and that has turned off many investors. Investors have moved to cash and bonds in an effort to avoid the volatility of stocks.

And that's a **mistake**. Stocks are the only asset class that over the long run will give you the returns necessary to avoid the ravages of inflation and taxes (and prison, in the case of offshore accounts). Don't pretend you're a rich man by opening a Swiss bank account. Take the safe bet and stick with equities.

Credit cards, debit cards and cash

In the developed world we are seeing a move away from a cash-based society to one that is solely focused on credit and debit cards. The developing world is just the opposite. **Cash is king**, and while there is a slow movement towards cards, I would advise you to rarely if ever use them. If you must use them, use your credit card rather than a debit card. Why? Every time you use a card of any kind, you risk an unnecessary charge being added to your bill, or even worse, your card being **cloned** and used by a thief. The latter has happened to me while living abroad. If you use a credit card, you can dispute the charges and not pay them. Credit card companies also tend to be more agreeable when it comes to reducing or removing charges. With debit cards, on the other hand, there are far fewer protections, and lost money **is taken directly out of your bank account**. Trying to convince a bank to put back money into your account is quite a challenge, particularly if it's a foreign bank.

Another issue with the use of cards is the fact that you have to rely on a working bank network. When you use a card to pay for a meal, the restaurant swipes the card in a scanner that dials your bank by phone to confirm whether it can charge for the meal. If your bank's network is down for the day due to technical difficulties, your card won't go through. **This is a common occurrence** in the developing world, even in upscale parts of the world like Dubai. You do not want to get stuck being unable to pay. Once again, cash is king.

Live like a local, not a westerner

If you try to live like a Westerner in your new country, unless you are wealthy, you will quickly run out of money. In my opinion, living like a westerner means buying **imported goods.** Unlike in the West, particularly the United States, countries cannot run up huge trade deficits and receive cheap goods from exporting countries like China. Instead they have to make do with what they have, and in order to protect their own industries, will typically slap tariffs on imported goods. The consequence of this is that things like **televisions, cars, computers, portable electronics and books** are very expensive relative to their cost in your home country. Whenever possible, I suggest going without them.

That means no television in **every room.** Only one car for your family, rather than one for every member. If possible, go without a car and use public transportation or be driven to destinations by a local. You might also skimp on the purchase of a dishwasher and dryer, and instead do it yourself or hire someone else to do it. Appliances are very expensive to purchase in most countries. If you **must** have a particular item, such as a computer, purchase it before you leave.

Practical Matters

Buy locally

In general, you should avoid buying anything **imported** when living abroad. Only in countries like the United States, and perhaps parts of Northern Europe, can you buy cheap imported goods. Most developing countries slap high tariffs on cheaply-produced goods from countries like China in order to protect their own industries. In plainer English, that means that locally-made goods will always be substantially cheaper than foreign products.

Buy locally means **eat locally** as much as possible too. Westerners would be shocked to realize that many of the tropical fruits and vegetables they eat back home are imported. To import an exotic fruit or vegetable to your new home in the developing world will be tremendously expensive. Learn to eat what the locals eat, and enjoy it. The more of your old life you import, the greater your expenses will be.

Learn to use products not sold in chain stores, such as so-called hypermarkets like Carre-four, Asda, Walmart, etc. but goods produced just down the street. For instance furniture built by a local artisan would be perfect for your home. When negotiating to rent a property (or if you're foolish, buying a property), the owner will always include furniture as part of the price. **Immediately say you do not want furniture**, and use that as a bargaining chip. You can easily replace beds, tables, chairs and rugs with goods produced locally for very little. It's exactly the same place the owner bought his furniture as well.

Alcohol is probably one of your biggest expenses if you decide to import it. If you insist on having your favorite beer or liquor every evening and it is imported, you can be sure to run into budget trouble. Try the local stuff and save money. Unlike drinking water from the tap, alcohol kills germs, and will probably be safe to drink regularly. Will it taste better than what you're used to? Who knows? If your consumption is reduced, all the better, for the sake of health. What is surprising about importing alcohol is how easy it is for people to forget how a mere drink can be so expensive. Unlike an appliance or furniture or a car, alcohol in terms of price per liter is extraordinarily expensive. In fact, far more expensive than almost anything you can think of that could be imported. Buy accordingly.

Air conditioning

Perhaps the most expensive thing you can splurge on is **air conditioning**. The current drawn by an air conditioning unit, particularly a centralized air conditioning system, is immense. For Americans, who are used to the constant flow of air conditioning, living without it is quite a challenge. For other westerners, air conditioning is also an expensive luxury.

A common alternative is **wall units** that are placed in every room that requires cooling. These have the advantage of being cheaper because instead of cooling the entire house, they cool only the room you are in. They have certain drawbacks, though. In my experience using them in the Persian Gulf, they tended to create moisture and drip water down the wall, peeling paint and if on the second floor of a house, dripping it into the room below. They also periodically break, and are not as **reliable** as central air.

The final alternative is of course a **fan**. An electric fan constantly blowing is not nearly as pleasant as air conditioning, but you can be confident that virtually everyone else in your new country is using one too. Air conditioning is a great expense. And with electricity somewhat intermittent, with **frequent blackouts** and brownouts during summer months because of poorly-built and overloaded local electrical systems, you will probably have to rely on a hand fan periodically anyway. My advice is to acclimatize yourself to living without air conditioning, particularly if the county you are moving to is known for an unreliable electricity supply.

Bribery and corruption

In the developing world, bribery is a part of life. In fact, in countries where it is rife, it is a significant part of the economy. Many times police forces make much of their salaries from local bribes that come in the form of "fines". These are arbitrary and on the surface will seem unfair. I would **avoid arguing** about them. The key I have found to bribing a policeman is to settle whatever issues there are right at the scene of the problem. Instead of demanding to go to the police station or to appear in front of a magistrate, **pay the bribe now**. By dealing with more police officers and public officials, you risk having to pay more "fines" and bribing many more people. The fewer people you bribe, the cheaper you can get off.

There is an interesting index known as the **Corruption Perception Index (CPI)**. The index is published each year by Transparency International, a German NGO that seeks to raise awareness about international corruption and the issues related to it. The index looks at "the degree to which corruption is perceived to exist among public officials and politicians" according to its website. Here are the top ten **least corrupt** countries, with the least corrupt at the top:

1. New Zealand
2. Denmark

3. Singapore
3. Sweden
5. Switzerland
6. Finland
6. Netherlands
8. Australia
8. Canada
8. Iceland

What is interesting is that in the top ten is a country that is by no means totally democratic (Singapore), and there are developed countries such as Italy scoring far lower than developing countries such as Uruguay and Chile. Dictatorships I have lived in, including Bahrain (46) and the UAE (30), score well, though I believe the index is overweighting **street-level corruption** which is low in those two countries, and underweighting **institutional corruption,** which is high there. I define street level corruption as the corruption a person faces on a daily basis. That would include the bribery of police, staff at a company, or any low-level civil servant to get what you need.

Institutional corruption I would define as corruption that allows the wealthy to do as they see fit, either due to the fact that they are related to or closely associated with government leaders, or because they are in fact the leaders of the government!

Street-level corruption is the corruption that **will affect you the most**. Because it involves dealing with police officers, taxi drivers, office staff, etc., it will put a strain on your daily budget. High levels of street level corruption are both a drain on the local economy and a **hidden tax**. They also require you to become skilled at **haggling**. You will need to bargain with police, taxi drivers will not use meters and will demand a deal for whatever route you want to take, shops will never give you a set price that is fair. For someone from a developed country, it can be **very exhausting**. If you are unused to such behavior you might wish to reconsider moving o these types of countries. Countries that that score in the 40s or higher on the CPI I would consider to have high levels of street level corruption, as well as institutional corruption.

Institutional corruption is what it sounds like. It is corruption of the major institutions that make up a country. This is far more prevalent than street-level corruption, and is far more **insidious**. It means that a person living in a country with high levels of institutional corruption will only be able to rise so far unless he or she is **related** to someone in power, or **knows** someone in power. It means there is little recourse if you wish to take on an institution you feel has wronged you. **The most common way expats get on the wrong side of institutional corruption is when they buy property.** When you buy a property in a corrupt country, you have little or no recourse if the property is defective, quickly loses its value, or has fees associated with it that rise dramatically.

The second most common way expats get on the wrong side of institutional corruption is when **they are employed in a corrupt country**. This will occur if they feel they have had their work visa arbitrarily revoked, that their employer has treated them unfairly, or that they have not been paid on time or at all. Usually they find that they have little or no recourse, particularly if their employer is a powerful organization within the country.

If you wish to avoid institutional corruption, the best thing you can do is to **limit your interaction with the government of that country.** That means involving yourself contractually only when absolutely necessary. Avoid signing property deeds, avoid contractual relationships with locals, and avoid having to tangle with any bureaucracy. Make use of your own embassy instead whenever possible. Of course filling out the forms necessary to rent a property, get a visa, and receive medical care are all things I highly recommend that you **do not avoid**.

Moral laws

Depending on where you come from in the world, you may have to adjust your behavior somewhat to your new country. What might be acceptable on a Friday night out after a few drinks could be seen as very **sinful behavior** in another country.

In my experience abroad, the most stark example that comes to mind was during my time in Dubai. A British couple was caught by Dubai police allegedly having sex on a beach late at night. After several months of house arrest, followed by considerable media scrutiny in the Gulf and in Britain, the pair were given a suspended sentence and deported. The woman, who worked in Dubai, was fired from her job. In most developed countries little would have occurred if the police had come upon the couple.

The biggest problems expatriates get into abroad are usually drug and alcohol-related. While alcohol use is tolerated in many countries, drug use is almost universally seen as a very **illegal act**. In countries like the United States, and some parts of Europe, marijuana has largely been decriminalized, or legalized for medicinal purposes. However, in most other parts of the world, its use is an act punishable by a severe sentence. Even in countries where it is widely done, it is a risky act.

The consequence of drug use being seen in such a negative light by the international community is that if you are caught using drugs, your home government may not assist you as strongly it would in the case of other crimes. There are thousands of Western expatriates languishing in third world prisons for drug offenses. The recent case of a British citizen expat executed at the end of 2009 in China demonstrates the willingness of the developing world to punish all drug users equally and brutally.

Overt displays of affection, vulgar gestures, spitting etc., these are all behaviors that must be minimized when traveling abroad. "Rights" are not universal. What you believe you have the "right" to do in public may not be allowed in every country.

Drugs and crime

Throughout the developing world, particularly in Latin America, drugs and the drug trade have taken an **immense** toll. Crime related to drugs, particularly in countries like Colombia and Mexico has skyrocketed. Currently, Ciudad Juarez, a large city in the north of Mexico, has the **highest murder rate** in the world, higher even than war zones such as Baghdad and Kabul.

An expat must realize that if he or she moves to Latin America, particularly Central America and Mexico, they are moving to countries that are at times extremely dangerous. In the case of Mexico, the most popular residential destination for Americans in the world, the drug war has destabilized the country, and made many northern cities **no-go zones**.

The Financial Guide to Working Overseas

In these areas, the Mexican government has all but ceded control to local drug lords.

The drug trade is a booming business that is growing by leaps and bounds due to the insatiable appetite for cocaine, marijuana and methamphetamine by Americans and to a lesser extent Canadians. Central America has become the largest conduit of drugs in the world into the United States. With cheaply grown drugs selling for hundreds of times what it cost to make them, the profits are **enormous** and have fueled drug empires stretching across the North and South American continents.

All of this has made a stay in much of Latin America more **problematic**. My suggestion is to stay away from cities that have been ceded to the drug cartels. Avoid using drugs yourself. And most importantly, learn what you can from expats in the know who can give you a better picture of what is really going on in the country.

In a country such as Mexico, the power vacuum created by drug lords displacing government control in certain regions has allowed a new type of criminal to emerge. **Kidnappers** are a potential threat to expats who make their home in Mexico, though they have by and large only targeted Mexicans and/or Americans of Mexican descent. Kidnapping has skyrocketed throughout Mexico, and people of means are being targeted. The purpose of these kidnappings is quite simple: **ransom.** For many criminals, the drug trade is either too competitive or not profitable enough, and in true entrepreneurial spirit, they have discovered a new and at times very profitable revenue stream. For expats, this means you should **watch out!**

Practical Matters

While the drug trade has increased crime throughout Latin America, it has not increased it to the extent that it has in Mexico. Other Latin American countries are still **relatively** safe destinations, for now.

Racism/Provincialism/Prejudice

Any discussion of moral laws must also coincide with a discussion about racism and prejudice. It is often the case that a poorer country will have provincial attitudes towards behaviors that are tolerated to a much greater extent in the developed world. When learning about your new country, determine through interviews with other expatriates whether they have experienced racism or any form of prejudice. The closer to your own ethnicity the expat you interview is, the better.

In many countries, what would be considered racism by some, would be seen as humorous by others. Throughout Latin America, and even in Spain, **caricatures** of blacks are found in cartoons and on the packaging of various foods and candies. These caricatures would be seen as deeply offensive in the United States and elsewhere. It is also common in Latin America to refer to someone by a prominent physical feature in a friendly way. This would be unacceptable in much of the developed world.

In my own experience as someone of mixed race heritage (I am half Mexican/half Scottish), I have found that the world is remarkably less racist than is commonly assumed. I myself have never experienced overt hatred for the way I look in my travels abroad. Of course my experience may be unique.

Much of what could be construed as racism is simply ignorance. There is also a difference between ignorance and overt hatred. Ignorance is common, while overt hatred against someone because of the way they look is uncommon. Virtually every ethnicity has examples of wealthy, successful individuals, and many of the old stereotypes that certain ethnic groups were poor, dumb and uncivilized have diminished as everyone in the world slowly emerges from poverty.

Homosexuality and living overseas

Gays and homosexuality in general are frowned upon in the more religious and poorer parts of the world. Sadly, many popular residential destinations in the developing world are **potentially unsafe or unfriendly** for gay men and women. While Mexico City has legalized gay marriage, much of the rest of Latin America has been slow to follow. Evo Morales, the President of Bolivia, recently discussed how the eating of hormone-fed chickens might be a leading cause of homosexuality, so you can imagine how well gays are viewed in that country.

I believe it is safe to assume that a country that allows gay marriage or civil unions is probably a safe destination for gay expats. As of the year 2010, the following countries around the world allow gay marriage: Sweden, South Africa, Norway, Canada, Spain, Belgium, South Africa and the Netherlands.

I consider countries that give the right of gay marriage to be more gay-friendly than countries that only allow **civil partnerships, common law marriages**, or other legal unions for gays. Legalizing gay marriage means that the local government has ignored the protests of religious leaders, and has given gay couples the same rights as straight couples, whereas a civil partnership is accepted only by the government and not by religious leaders.

Practical Matters

The following countries as of the year 2010 allow some sort of civil partnership for gay couples: Hungary, Austria, **France**, Ecuador, **Australia**, **Uruguay**, **Switzerland**, Slovenia, Andorra, Luxembourg, **New Zealand**, **Portugal,** Germany, the United Kingdom and Denmark.

The following countries as of the year 2010 allow for common law gay marriages: Czech Republic and **Croatia**.

A civil partnership has **more** legal weight than a common law marriage. Traditionally, a common law marriage simply meant that a couple was considered married if they had cohabited for a period of time. You can see how that might result in legal problems if you have difficulty proving cohabitation for whatever reason. You could rightly view a country that has only legalized gay common law marriages as one with **inferior** gay rights protections, compared to one where gay civil unions or even gay marriages are legal.

Essentially, gay-friendly countries fall into a **five tier** system: countries that allow gay marriage, countries that allow civil unions, countries that allow common law marriages, and finally **countries that prohibit gay marriage, and countries that prohibit homosexuality** altogether.

The two bottom tiers are countries that gays should approach warily. Typically, countries outside of Western Europe either give gay people fewer rights, or openly discriminate against them. My advice to a gay person **is to avoid countries that openly discriminate against gays**. These countries are typically found in sub-Saharan Africa, and parts of Asia. They are also typically found in Muslim countries as well.

Of course gay people are everywhere, even in countries where homosexuality is prohibited. As I am not gay, I am unable to give a clear picture of which countries tolerate homosexuality more than others. I will say that in countries where it is prohibited, you can expect to find no **clubs or bars** out in the open for gay clientele. In countries where homosexuality is tolerated but gay rights are not protected, you may be hard-pressed to find establishments that openly cater to gays. In all of these countries there is the potential for violence against gays, and the arbitrary closing down of establishments that secretly serve gay customers.

The treatment of women

For the female expat, moving abroad in many ways is more of a danger and a challenge than it is for a man. That is not to say that a woman can't find **immense enjoyment** from living abroad. I simply think that a woman should tread a little more carefully, particularly in the developing world. Women's rights are new to much of the globe, and the status of women in most societies is, unfortunately, not equal to that of men.

How do you measure how well a country treats women? You can look at various elements such as access to education for women, whether women have the right to vote, and how large pay gaps are between men and women. Are there many female political leaders in the country you are looking at? How long is female life expectancy versus male life expectancy? Are women dying in childbirth at alarming rates? All of these factors play a role in determining the status of women in a country.

While some of the poorest and most religious countries in the world tend to discriminate against women horrendously, many of the countries in this guide are either strong in the area of women's rights, or are progressing

Practical Matters

well. The United Nations has developed an index, the **Gender-related Development Index (GDI),** that takes the mathematical equations that are the foundation of the famous Human Development Index and adds many of the statistical factors affecting women that I wrote about in the previous paragraph. Below are the top ten countries on the list as of **2009**:

1. Sweden
2. Norway
3. Finland
4. Denmark
5. Netherlands
6. Belgium
7. Australia
8. Iceland
9. Germany
10. New Zealand

Northern European countries dominate the list at the top. The rest of Europe fills out most of the remainder of the top 30 spots. Latin America would be the second highest region on the list, followed Asia and then the Middle East. Some countries, particularly those from Africa are not listed because of insufficient data. For the complete list in a downloadable pdf, use this link:

http://hdr.undp.org/en/media/HDR_2009_EN_Table_K.pdf

It goes without saying that the less developed and more impoverished a country is, in general, the more likely the country will have fewer opportunities for women and a greater disparity in between the genders.

Disabled access

If you have mobility issues due to a handicap, or are in any way disabled, you may find it difficult to live in many countries, particularly if they are poor. While developed countries have passed **laws** guaranteeing that many businesses must allow access to disabled customers, the age of many buildings makes implementing these laws difficult. Oftentimes a business will conform to the law, but just enough not to get into trouble. Such a result is hardly ideal.

To a disabled reader, or someone with a disabled spouse or family member, living abroad will be fraught with difficulties. Obviously, Europe and the United States will have the best facilities available as in both areas there are laws mandating **accessibility**. The more exotic locales will probably be out of bounds for many with disabilities.

If you wish to live in the developing world, some of the wealthier countries in Latin America such as Uruguay, Argentina, Mexico and Costa Rica will have more accessible restaurants and hotels, but finding an apartment or house to rent will be difficult. Check with real estate brokers to find residences with previous owners/renters who had mobility issues similar to yours.

Sadly, there is little in the way of information on the internet for disabled expats overseas. The stereotypical expat is seen as someone who doesn't require anything in the way of special treatment and the dilemmas facing disabled expats are ignored. There is useful information for traveling abroad as a disabled person, but little in the way of information on permanent living abroad for disabled people.

Practical Matters

My suggestion is to research and find out whether the country you wish to move to requires businesses to have handicapped access. Find out if services are available to help with mobility issues through the use of specially equipped vehicles to transport you. Poor countries often expect the extended family to take care of someone who is disabled, and this is not often an option for a disabled person from a western country. In our part of the world government fills the gap.

Any move overseas for a disabled person will mean spending more money than the average expat will have to spend, in order to modify living quarters for accessibility. The cost savings found in the developing world can be rapidly eaten up through the employment of staff and to pay for changes to living space. My final suggestion is to permanently avoid moving to the poorest countries in the world, and to be prepared to not skimp on your budget in order overcome any challenges your new environment might present.

Street Crime

Crime is a very complex topic, and though it is a crucially important one, I can only touch upon it briefly here. In general, crime is low in the developed world, and high in the developing world (the United States is the notable exception). There is **overwhelming** evidence that the leading cause of crime is **poverty**.

If you move to the developing world, you can expect to at some point be a **victim** of crime. The greatest reason for crime is poverty, and the developing world is filled with impoverished souls. But what kind of crime do you have to fear? Most likely your residence will be targeted by thieves while you are away or you will be pickpocketed.

The same basic rules for keeping your home safe apply anywhere. Avoid leaving your cars or bicycles on the street. Lock all doors and windows. Buy an alarm system, as even the sound of it going off may scare away some thieves. But most importantly, don't let anyone know you have valuables, and if you have them, store them in as safe a place as possible. Thieves target those who appear to have money, and if you live far better than the rest of the population and regularly wear jewelry in public, you can expect to be targeted.

Having a criminal background

If you have a criminal background, you may have trouble qualifying to live in any foreign country. If the crime you committed was years ago, you **might** be able to be allowed to enter. If the crime is a minor one where you served only a brief time in jail, you **might** be let in. It all depends on the staff at the embassy/consulate/immigration board that is conducting the review and how they read the relevant laws that day.

In general, have a clean record. In today's hi-tech world, a background check can uncover virtually any dirt from your past. What you served time for and have all but forgotten about will seem like yesterday to an immigration officer. There are no repercussions for getting rejected because of a bad background, unless you are a fugitive, but if one country rejects you, expect all the rest to as well.

Alcoholism

One of the most pressing problems for expatriate communities around the world is the issue of alcoholism. Alcoholism is an insidious disease that strongly affects expats for several reasons. For one, some expat cultures have always promoted alcoholic consumption, and these expats have

Practical Matters

brought their problem with them. People from **colder climates** tend to drink far more than people from **warmer ones**. What may have been a worthwhile habit to combat cold and damp weather can quickly become a debilitating illness in a warm and alcohol-plentiful environment.

What expats who drink regularly need to understand is that they may at times be considered by locals to be drunks who can be taken advantage of, or to be a source of offense to the conservative locals. Many cultures look down on excessive drinking, or for that matter, drinking at all. Consider carefully whether your drinking could be a source of trouble for you in your new country.

Another popular cause of alcoholism is **boredom**. While you may have visited your expatriate paradise in the past, you only stayed for a short period of time, no longer than two weeks. It never occurred to you that lying on a hammock day after day listening to the waves hit the beach could be so mind-numbing. To compensate, you drink. What was never an issue before in your life has become deadly.

Lack of activities is the leading cause of boredom. Many island nations or beach communities will in some sense **lack culture**. By this I mean that the local movie theater with subtitled or dubbed Hollywood action films will be your only cultural outlet. Many expats assume that immersion in a new culture is itself enough to keep your mind busy. It is not. When you move to that isolated beach or mountain, you are essentially moving to a place where most locals **do not want to live**. They've all moved to the city for jobs and culture. You have moved to what they **abandoned.** Keeping busy with hobbies, sports and trips is the best way to stay away from the bottle.

Hiring help

If you decide to move to the developing world, you will find that the cost of labor is cheap enough that you will be able to afford housekeepers, and possibly a driver and other assistants. The easiest way to find a housekeeper is to ask your fellow expatriates who they use. They should be able to recommend someone.

When hiring someone to clean up after you, I suggest asking them to come only **once or twice a week**. Putting up someone in your home on a permanent basis requires substantial attention to that person's issues and problems. You'll need to supply him or her with furniture, food, bed linens, etc. A weekly or bi-weekly cleaning is enough for any lifestyle, and allows you to save on expenses. My experience with this type of hired help has been great. I would also include the washing of clothes in your helper's duties, but not ironing unless you are physically unable to iron yourself. Any clothes that require dry cleaning such as dress shirts, suits and other clothing should be kept in a place where the housekeeper cannot accidentally wash them and ruin them.

Sadly, when items are stolen the most likely culprit will be your hired help. Conceal valuables well. Even if your housekeeper has no intention of stealing from you, but mentions offhand to a friend the beautiful necklace she saw around your wife's neck before you went off to dinner, such an act can result in thievery. You must take extra precautions in an impoverished country. As a westerner you will be seen as wealthy whether you are or not. Plan accordingly. Complain constantly about how poor you are, even if it isn't true.

Practical Matters

As you get older and perhaps more infirm, the need for high-quality assistance becomes even greater. In the developing world, nurses can be hired cheaply, while in other developed countries in Western Europe and in places like New Zealand and Australia, the health services will provide high-quality health assistance, provided you can afford local insurance or are qualified for the public healthcare. My point here is that you must make sure that your nurses are from **reliable** and **trustworthy** sources. It is one thing for a housekeeper to steal from you; it is quite another for a nurse to take advantage of you when you are most vulnerable.

Moving your stuff

One of the biggest issues when moving abroad is the actual moving itself. The logistics involved in moving to another country are immense. I have a suggestion that may seem brutal to some readers, but I feel it is a necessary one: **move as little stuff as possible**.

In today's disposable society, we all have a tendency to **hoard** mementos and such. As a westerner you are probably used to having a large wardrobe, a large set of dishes and tableware, and huge, comfortable beds. If you move the developing world, or if you are an American moving anywhere outside of the United States, you can expect to have to put up with smaller appliances, beds, rooms, houses etc.

In fact, if you move your stuff from home you may find it **incompatible** with your new country. **Voltage** is the most obvious example. Various countries use various voltages, and you will need adapters to run all your various gadgets. As we grow to depend on high tech "appliances" like Blackberries and laptops, changing voltage might result in the destruction of your device.

What is perhaps not as obvious is that moving things like **beds** can entail similar difficulties. Mattress sizes are not uniform throughout the world. Bed frames that are purchased locally may not fit your mattress, nor will locally-made sheets. Cars from abroad may use too much gas, or use the wring kind of fuel entirely. In Egypt natural gas is one of the more common fuels for cars. In Brazil ethanol is the most popular fuel. Your car may have to be converted at considerable expense.

The key to successfully living abroad is to live like a local as much as is both **reasonable** and **possible**. If you move to a developing country I don't mean that you must live in a shack with no running water. But I do mean that you should seek to copy the lifestyles of a local from the upper middle class and, only if you can afford it, the upper class. What constitutes upper middle class varies from country to country, but it means someone who takes full advantage of the low cost of living, and what is locally produced and manufactured.

Pets are a considerable issue when moving. Be aware that many countries, particularly those that are islands and/or have unique ecosystems that the introduction of a feral pet might affect will probably require you to **quarantine** your pet for a period of time.

Clothes

When it comes to dress when living in your new country, I suggest two rules. One, dress in such a way as to **not offend**. Two, dress as much **like the locals** as possible.

In terms of not offending, I would suggest that you dress according to the environment you are in. Beach wear should be worn solely at the beach in conservative countries. While going without a shirt and shoes (if male), or in only a swimsuit (if female) would be more permissible in a European or American setting, in other countries in the developing world it would be frowned upon. Your goal at all times should be to blend in, and not stand out, as you are a **guest** of sorts in your new country. Wearing what you feel is most comfortable can not only offend, it can also make you a target for crime, as it will reveal to others that you are a "well-off westerner".

I also think you should dress like a local as much as is possible. Locals will buy locally-made clothes which **are cheaper**, in fact far cheaper, than imported clothes. Locally-made clothes will also be more comfortable and be made to withstand **local weather**. And again, looking like a local will make you look like less of a tourist/outsider and more like someone who fits in, which will help you avoid being targeted for crime.

There's one big problem with buying clothes locally, however. **They may not fit**. As a westerner you are probably much bigger and taller than the locals. Shoes are probably one of the biggest issues, and shoes that fit big feet are hard to find outside the western world. You may be forced to make a regular trip home to restock on clothes if you have too large a frame for local clothes. Fortunately, in the developing world **hand-tailored** clothes are remarkably cheap and can be made for your size. All my suits were hand-tailored in Bahrain, cost less than 100 US dollars apiece, and have impeccable stitching. Materials, though, are not world-class but are decent.

Phone plans

When living abroad, the general rule concerning phone plans is to avoid using long distance as much as possible, and make use of local phones for local calls.

Voice over Internet Protocol (VoIP) companies, such as Skype, are the best solution to making long distance phone calls. If you use a VoIP company you will save a great deal of money. However, the problem with VoIP is that the **sound quality** is not good if you call with a regular landline from your computer. Using VoIP to call another person/computer using VoIP results in very good call quality, though. I have been in a situation where I was using VoIP to call a business in another country to save money, and I was apparently very difficult to understand to the other caller. Because the other caller was not tech-savvy, and did not make use of VoIP himself, I was forced to use a cell phone for an international call at considerable expense. If you make regular use of a VoIP system, be sure to buy the best possible **headset and microphone** in order to maximize the quality of your internet calls.

VoIP is a necessity in much of the developing world where corrupt governments have allowed a monopoly or near-monopoly to take control of the phone system and charge exorbitant rates. But for local calls, it is a nuisance as it is far more troublesome to make a phone call from your computer than from a phone. The newest cell phones coming onto the market have VoIP options, but they only work if you are in the vicinity of a Wi-Fi network.

Since you are largely dependent on the local cellular network to make local calls, I suggest **texting** as a cheap alternative to making an actual call. While texting might be seen as something teenagers do obsessively, it is a reasonable alternative to calls once you learn to type fast enough. Be careful not to say anything sensitive on your texts, as the phone company records them all!

Relationships

An in-depth discussion about relationships and moving overseas is too involving for the subject matter of this book but it is an important enough issue that it deserves some discussion. It is my firm opinion that **you cannot live successfully abroad if your significant other is not on board**. I have seen firsthand relationships falter because one partner was unhappy living overseas. It is essential that both members of a relationship are keen to move abroad and work together.

Moving overseas for work is often done because only good opportunities are available in foreign countries for many people. When situations like that occur, the other spouse is often dragged along against his or her will. That's when the trouble starts. If you add excessive drinking, a change in work schedules, or a radical change in lifestyle to the mix, you have a recipe for disaster. Moving overseas is a jarring experience. It is better suited for some personalities rather than others. Make sure your significant other is happy and adjusting well. While one party may be very interested in the new environment, don't let exploring your new surroundings make you forget about the needs of your partner.

The Financial Guide to Working Overseas

Chapter Seven – Healthcare

In my opinion, there's nothing more important to human happiness than **good health**. Quite simply, poor health prevents you from accomplishing your goals, will swallow up your time, and possibly leave you **destitute**. It's for these reasons that an in-depth discussion about healthcare is a necessity for any book about working and living abroad.

Employer health insurance

For most people who work overseas, you will be given health insurance from your employer. This health insurance will more than likely be comprehensive, allow for some elective procedures, and have a dental plan attached. While your health insurance will in all likelihood be supplied by your employer, you need to understand that the healthcare you receive abroad may be in many ways inferior, more expensive, and/or even not guaranteed to cover you in the event of an emergency.

The importance of comprehensive healthcare insurance

The entire developed world, including the United States by 2014, offers comprehensive health insurance to all its citizens. Much of the developing world offers it as well, though it typically is lacking in quality compared with the healthcare offered by wealthier nations. However, as a foreign resident, you most likely will not qualify for this public plan. Instead you will be dependent on private insurance or your own money to pay for any healthcare.

You never know when something might happen to you that will require you to make a hospital stay. It is because of this that comprehensive healthcare insurance is essential. Don't skimp on this area, even if paying out of pocket for healthcare is affordable for you. A critical injury, a long hospital stay, or extensive surgery all will mean thousands of dollars in expenses if you don't have insurance.

The basic rules for healthcare insurance

I am assuming that the audience for this book is made up of people from the developing world seeking to move overseas either to other developed countries, or to the developing world. This means that everyone reading this book has access to high quality healthcare in their home country if they require it. With that in mind, here are my basic rules for having healthcare when living abroad:

- **Keep your home healthcare insurance, no matter what.** If you live abroad, and you come down with a chronic condition and your only healthcare is private, you might very well be dropped by your health insurance or not be given all the necessary treatments as the hospital or insurance company looks to save money. By keeping your home health insurance (which is probably run by the government, like Medicare or the NHS), you have the backup option of being flown out of the country and receiving free high-quality treatment. **Unregulated** private insurers are about profits first, treatment second. Private health insurance that you get abroad, particularly in the developing world, is unregulated, and may drop you if you become too expensive. So, if your home country's health insurance won't cover you if you do not keep up with the payments, or will charge you more if you get back on their coverage as Medicare in the USA does, I strongly suggest you keep up with your payments. Remember the saying: **penny wise, pound foolish**.

- **Don't be afraid of a developed country's public healthcare system**. This section is written primarily for American readers. Many Americans are under the mistaken belief that government-issued healthcare is inferior or terrible, and they pay through the nose for additional private healthcare even when they are eligible for the local government healthcare. A key indicator of the effectiveness of a country's public healthcare is the country's life expectancy and infant mortality. Such statistics are readily available on the internet. The better the numbers, the more reliable the local healthcare has to be.
- **Look for high deductible, low premium plans**. In most countries, particularly those of the developing world, healthcare is inexpensive for basic things like doctor's visits, x-rays, and generic prescriptions. The more you pay out of pocket, the more

reasonable your insurance costs will be. The higher the deductible, the lower the premium, which means the lower the monthly payment and less of an impact on your budget. If you are a healthy person, and rarely need to see a doctor, this could be to your advantage. I'm not advocating not seeing a doctor, I'm simply looking at this from a budgetary point of view. Insurance companies will view you as less of a health risk if they see that you are willing to pay more upfront. If you have a condition which requires regular medical attention, a low deductible plan is the better option, but you will pay for higher premiums.

Do I need medical evacuation insurance?

It's common for many expats living overseas to have health insurance with an option to evacuate them back to their home country for treatment in the event of a **serious** health emergency. The idea behind this insurance is that if you are living in a poorer country, and you have something really bad happen to you such as a coma or a stroke, you will want the best treatment available and that means treatment back home, safely in the warm embrace of advanced western medicine. I think there are times when this insurance is worth it, and I think there are times when it is **overkill**.

If you live in a developed country, I wouldn't bother, especially if you qualify for the publicly funded health insurance. The healthcare locally is world class, particularly in Western European countries such as France and Italy. In the developing world, you may want to consider purchasing it.

What a lot of expats don't understand is that their private healthcare, unless local laws say otherwise, **is not guaranteed**. That means that if you end up in a coma and your hospitalization is costing your health insurer a lot of money, they might drop you in the middle of treatment. An evacuation policy is a way out of this dilemma. By being evacuated back to your home country you can make use of your government-backed healthcare, which, as I warned before, you should do everything you can to keep.

Some might also consider holding evacuation insurance, and not getting local health insurance. That would mean paying for any local doctor visits **out of pocket**. I'm not sure if I can recommend this. As an American, I have seen firsthand what insurance companies are capable of if they are not ordered by the government to cover people under any circumstances.

If they can, they will drop you. I am a firm believer in having as many backups as is reasonable and possible. That means having good local health insurance, in addition to having an evacuation plan, and keeping your eligibility for your country's government-subsidized health insurance as well.

So which countries have the best healthcare systems?

The **World Health Organization (WHO)**, perhaps the world's leading health NGO, ranked in 2000 the healthcare systems of all of the world's countries. This ranking is the most recent, and it is unclear if the WHO will update the rankings, but the list remains the best comparative analysis of every country's ability to insure the health of its citizens and legal residents. Below are the top ten countries:

1. France
2. Italy

3. San Marino
4. Andorra
5. Malta
6. Singapore
7. Spain
8. Oman
9. Austria
10. Japan
11. Norway
12. Portugal
32. Australia
41. New Zealand

As is typical with lists like these, we find that the leading countries all have very high cost of living and are mostly in the developed world. But it gives you a clearer picture as to where the countries with the best healthcare are. In the first 30 spots on the list, almost every country is located within Western Europe. The United States is ranked 37th.

The full list can be found at this website as a downloadable pdf:

http://www.who.int/whr/2000/en/whr00_en.pdf

What causes a country to be ranked higher or lower? Basically, a country is ranked according to its efficacy at giving healthcare to all its people. That doesn't necessarily mean that a country is incapable of having good healthcare, it just means that only those who can afford it have any access. When moving to a country that ranks low on this WHO list, consider whether you will be able to afford top-tier healthcare there. If you can't, you might want to reconsider the country. You don't want to be on the bottom rung, with that country's poor.

How to find high-quality healthcare in a country

That is not to say that there aren't high quality healthcare facilities in the developing world. In countries such as Mexico, Panama, and Argentina, there exist world class facilities. **Joint Commission International** (JCI) is an American not-for-profit organization that accredits healthcare providers in the United States and throughout the world. **Accredited** hospitals and clinics are allegedly supposed to deliver the highest levels of healthcare to patients.

There is **skepticism** as to how **trustworthy** these accreditations are, as hospitals pay to have them done. I would discuss with your nearest embassy or consulate as to what hospitals they recommend for treatment in your new country. Below is a list of JCI-accredited hospitals found in a variety of countries. You'll notice that larger countries with bigger economies have more hospitals. More hospitals means more spending on healthcare and more likelihood of being able to treat rare illnesses. The following countries have at least one hospital or medical facility accredited by JCI. Some have one, while others have dozens. Check with JCI's website to determine the current status of hospitals' accreditation around the world. Accreditation requires renewal, so checking with JCI will tell you whether a hospital is still maintaining its accreditation with the organization. Below are the countries with JCI accredited facilities:

1. Austria
2. Bahamas
3. Bangladesh

The Financial Guide to Working Overseas

4. Barbados
5. Belgium
6. Brazil
7. Chile
8. China
9. Colombia
10. Costa Rica
11. Cyprus
12. Czech Republic
13. Denmark
14. Egypt
15. Ethiopia
16. Germany
17. Greece
18. India
19. Indonesia
20. Ireland
21. Israel
22. Italy
23. Japan
24. Jordan
25. Lebanon
26. Mexico
27. Nicaragua
28. Pakistan
29. Philippines
30. Portugal
31. Qatar
32. Saudi Arabia

33. Singapore
34. Spain
35. South Korea
36. Switzerland
37. Taiwan
38. Thailand
39. Turkey
40. UAE
41. Vietnam
42. Yemen

These accreditations should only be viewed as the beginning of your investigation into finding high-quality healthcare in the country you move to. You should ask expats about their experiences and if possible tour hospital facilities yourself.

Don't fear public healthcare in the developed world

Healthcare in the developed world is generally excellent. A recent ranking of Western healthcare systems by the Commonwealth Fund ranked several Western nations, including New Zealand, Australia, Canada, Germany, UK, and the Netherlands, as surpassing the United States in several different metrics. The study confirms the WHO's ranking of several years ago, and shows that the commitment of Western democracies to providing high quality health care to their citizens is still at the forefront of their responsibilities. Be confident in depending on them. If your private healthcare fails to provide for every service provided by local doctors in a western country, it is highly unlikely that treatment will be withheld as there are generally laws that prevent hospitals from stopping treatment on those who can't afford it.

Be afraid of public healthcare in parts of the developing world, if it even exists

Unfortunately, public healthcare in poor countries is generally, well, poor. If you depend on it, you can expect lengthy waiting times for treatment and poor treatment when you get it. Many doctors in the developing world are required to work a certain amount of hours for the public, but the real money and bulk of their income comes from their private treatments. In such conditions, a doctor will undoubtedly be more likely to work harder for a patient that pays him or her more. Those without private health insurance will likely miss out on the best treatment, or in the worst cases, will miss out on treatment altogether.

Such is the tradeoff for living in an affordable country. Your healthcare will not be guaranteed, and treatment may stop if you run out of money, with potentially lethal consequences. If you choose to live in the developing world, make sure you can afford private healthcare, and make sure your healthcare back home is up to date and paid for.

Vaccinations and malarial regimens

Probably the smartest way to avoid illness is to get vaccinated. Depending on which country you move to, however, you will need **different** vaccinations, as the diseases occurring in certain countries occur because of the climate and the environment. For instance, **malaria** is a disease carried by mosquitoes and found only in tropical and subtropical parts of the world. It is not found often in the developed world, because most of the developed world is in **cold and temperate** climates.

Healthcare

If you move to a warmer and lusher climate, you can expect to face more and different diseases than you are used to. The world is a selfish place, and diseases that affect wealthier countries are the diseases that are cured first. It is for this reason that diseases that are unique to the developing world are a **constant and pervasive threat**, and there is often no cure in sight. Plan accordingly.

I have compiled below from a variety of pertinent medical sources a list of the most popular destinations for expats, as well as the necessary vaccinations for those destinations. **Be sure to check with your doctor for the final say in determining whether these vaccinations are right for you. As I have no idea what your medical history is, I cannot have any idea whether you will have an adverse reaction to the vaccinations I have listed below. This is simply a general guide that serves as a starting point for your preparation to move abroad. Always check with your healthcare provider for final word on vaccinations for travel.**

1. The Caribbean

In general, the Caribbean is seen as an area where destination-specific vaccinations are not recommended. There are two **notable exceptions,** Haiti and the Dominican Republic. It is recommended that you begin a malaria regimen before going to either of those countries, particularly if you plan to visit rural areas.

For all other Caribbean destinations, a standard Hepatitis A, Typhoid, Tetanus, and Polio vaccination set should be done.

2. Central America

In **Mexico**, **Belize**, **Costa Rica**, **Nicaragua** and in many parts of **Panama** a malaria risk is present. Rural areas, particularly those with considerable jungle flora, have a considerable threat of malaria, urban centers less so. A standard Hepatitis A, Typhoid, Tetanus, and Polio vaccination set should be done as well.

3. South America

In rural parts of **Argentina,** particularly in the north of the country near the borders with Paraguay and Bolivia, there is a malarial risk. The two other popular retirement locales of **Uruguay** and **Chile** have no malarial risk. **Brazil** has some malarial risk in all areas, particularly in the Amazon basin and other rural locations. A **yellow fever** vaccination is also recommended for Brazil, particularly for visits to the Amazon and other rural areas. A standard Hepatitis A, Typhoid, Tetanus, and Polio vaccination set should be done as well.

4. East Asia

In some rural parts of **Thailand**, there is a malarial risk. Urban centers are malaria-free. **Vietnam** is a malarial risk in the entire country. A standard Hepatitis A, Typhoid, Tetanus, and Polio vaccination set should be done as well. More developed and colder climates require only standard vaccinations.

5. Oceania

Australia has no malarial risk, and only a Tetanus vaccine is recommended. **New Zealand** has no malarial risk, and only a Tetanus vaccine is recommended.

6. Europe

No vaccinations are necessary other than Tetanus. A combination of developed-world status and a cold to temperate climate has made this part of the world safe from malaria and other tropical illnesses.

For further information consult www.traveldoctor.co.uk, or the US State Department website. Consult your **primary care** physician for final advice.

The Financial Guide to Working Overseas

Chapter Eight – Taxes

For most expats who wish to work abroad, taxes should be a significant consideration in where you choose to work. International taxation is an extremely complex subject, but I will endeavor to give a general overview of the major tax issues facing expats who work overseas. I will also discuss briefly the issues facing Americans, who are the only citizens in the western world who are forced to both submit an income tax return **and** pay taxes on their worldwide income **no matter where in the world they live.**

Tax havens

Not every country in the world taxes its citizens and residents. There are many countries in the world that have no income taxes at all for residents, and I have been fortunate enough to have lived in two of them (Bahrain and the UAE), so I have some experience dealing with international taxes in this area. For most expats a tax haven means, literally, no taxes to be paid at all. Though some publications define a tax haven as a place with little or no taxes, I define it as a place with **no income tax**. This book is primarily for working expats, and the vast majority of expats move abroad not to start businesses but to earn a wage. Thus the discussion below is primarily about countries and territories that do not tax the income of their residents.

However, a tax haven is never all it's made out to be. Though you will not pay taxes at all, you will likely have to deal with employers who take this into account and will offer you **a correspondingly lower salary**. Remember to take this into account if you decide to work in a tax haven.

The following countries and territories have no income tax for legal residents as of 2009-2010:

1. Andorra
2. Anguilla (British overseas territory)
3. Bahamas
4. Bahrain
5. Bermuda (British overseas territory)
6. Brunei (no income tax, but there is a 23.5 per cent corporate tax)
7. Cayman Islands (British overseas territory)
8. Kuwait
9. Liechtenstein
10. Monaco
11. Oman
12. Qatar

13. Saudi Arabia (only 2.5 per cent income tax rate)
14. UAE

Other countries will have special laws that allow an expat to avoid taxation on all **foreign income**. However, if you earn money in the country, you can expect to pay tax on that local income.

Tax treaties

A tax treaty is essentially an agreement between two countries that coordinates the taxation of individuals who may have the citizenship of one country and work in the other. Probably the best example of a set of tax treaties are the laws that regulate taxation between European countries in the EU. These tax treaties allow European citizens to move easily and freely between countries with little taxation difficulty. Tax treaties are created to help improve trade relations and make the movement of workers easier to accomplish.

For Americans, it is essential that you know if the country you are moving to has a tax treaty with the United States. This will help prevent **double taxation**. Double means you owe income taxes to the country you currently work in, as well as to the United States. Fortunately, the United States has tax treaties with many of the world's largest economies. Unfortunately, the United States does not have tax treaties with the rest of the world's countries. While the US does not tax income below a certain threshold (your first $91,400 of income is exempt as of 2010), anything over that is subject to taxation.

Estate taxes

If there is one way to run into trouble after you're gone, it is to buy property or other significant investments in another country. While I cannot go into the ramifications of estate taxes in every country listed as an ideal retirement destination in this book, I can say that if you purchase property overseas, there is a significant **danger** of having to pay estate taxes on that property in order to transfer it to heirs.

If you die **intestate** (without a will) and you own property overseas the local laws will apply and those laws may not be to your liking. Some jurisdictions may favor children over your spouse, or vice versa. If you are remarried and your children would like your property, you can expect a protracted fight between parties. More developed countries tend to have far larger estate taxes than developing countries as well.

The goal is to avoid **complexity**. Owning property in several countries means dealing with several legal systems, and far more issues and problems. No one is intimately familiar with several legal systems at once, not even attorneys. Avoid unnecessary entanglements by keeping the majority of your estate in one country and writing a will that makes this apparent for jurisdictional purposes in the event of a potential lawsuit after you have died.

Wealth taxes

Some countries have what is commonly known as a **wealth tax**. It is literally a tax on a person's collected wealth. This usually covers bank accounts, property, stocks, ownership stakes in companies, bonds, anything that is worth anything and could be considered part of a person's net worth. While other countries do not have a wealth tax per se, the fact that many of these assets are taxed separately constitutes a form of wealth tax as well.

Currently the following countries have wealth taxes that I am aware of:

1. India
2. Hungary
3. France
4. Norway
5. Netherlands
6. Liechtenstein
7. Switzerland

If you are working in these countries and have substantial assets, contact a local accountant or other tax professional to help you make sense of wealth taxes. My understanding is that wealth taxes pertain to what you own **in the country** not outside it.

The issues with domiciles

The key to avoiding double taxation or minimizing taxation while abroad is to avoid being **domiciled** in places where you face taxes. Domiciled is a vague way of saying that you have "roots" in a jurisdiction, and countries will use any evidence of a person being domiciled in their jurisdiction as proof that they are subject to taxation. What kind of roots are countries looking for? Property, time spent in the country, ownership of companies and the list goes on.

If you are living in a tax haven, or another country with a lower tax rate, or simply don't want to face double taxation, you should endeavor to avoid being domiciled in more than one place at once. The British government has recently become concerned that British citizens are buying small apartments in Monaco (because that is all that is available) and then moving to their big house in France on the weekends but taking full advantage of their residency in Monaco for tax avoidance purposes.

It's obvious that such a loophole would aggravate not only the British authorities, but the French ones as well. French property taxes are quite high, and a Monaco residency is often used to avoid them.

Tax law is extremely complex, and I cannot possibly speak expertly on the intricacies of tax law of three different countries. But I think there are general rules that apply to anyone who wishes to take advantage of a tax haven. I have lived in two different tax havens, Dubai and Bahrain, and am somewhat familiar with the basic rules that are required in order to take advantage of tax haven status.

In general your home country, the country that wishes to tax you, is looking to make sure that you are not still domiciled in any way back home. If you are, you can expect to have to pay tax. The tax authorities are looking to make sure that you are actually residing abroad in the tax haven most or all of the time.

Below is a list of ways to accomplish this:

1. Spend as much time as you possibly can in the tax haven itself. Minimize or completely negate spending anytime back home in the country that can tax you. Make use of video conferencing and phone systems to make up for the lack of time spent at home.

Taxes

2. The article above talks about "social" and "domestic" ties counting against you if you are trying to change your domicile. This is very broad language. It means that not only must you reside in the tax haven, you must not have substantial assets in your home taxable country. Your case is stronger if you sell the property you have back home, and any other assets such as cars and vacation homes.

3. Set up a real and permanent address in the tax haven country. You must establish that you are actually living there, not that you are merely using the cheapest address possible to qualify for tax avoidance status.

4. Make sure any family members who pay tax with you are complying with the same restrictions.

Again, I am no legal expert on international tax matters, but the more evidence that you can bring forth that you have completely severed ties with your home country, the better. Obviously the tax authorities are going after the big fish first, but don't think because you make less money you are not vulnerable. If anything you are more vulnerable as you don't have the money to defend yourself against a tax suit from back home.

My feeling is that we are entering into an era of **heightened restrictions** on tax avoidance. Offshore accounts and tax havens will fall under more and more scrutiny as the collateral damage from this most recent global financial crisis continues to grow. Governments are desperate for more tax revenues, and if an entire class of people is leaving the country and living abroad in a tax loophole, governments are going to make it as tough as possible for them to avoid taxation.

How to invest if you live in a tax haven

If you're lucky enough to live in a part of the world with no income taxes, and most importantly no capital gains taxes, congratulations! Investing will be very easy for you.

The problem is that you will have to decide before you invest **which country you plan on retiring in**. Why? Because if you decide to retire in Britain, but invest primarily in the United States because you are earning money in a country that has a currency pegged to the dollar (like most of the Persian Gulf is), you may very well suffer in the long run due to currency fluctuations between the dollar and the pound.

If you live in a tax haven like the GCC you should invest primarily in the US market (unless you plan on retiring in the Euro Zone or Britain). Why? Because all of the GCC (with the exception of Kuwait) has its currencies pegged to the dollar. In order to alleviate any currency fluctuations between the dollar and the rest of the world, it's best that you put your nest egg in American companies and bonds.

The easiest way to accomplish this is to open a brokerage account with an American stockbroker (choose the cheapest, it doesn't matter!) and simply buy ETFs that mirror the returns of the biggest indexes. I suggest Vanguard's ETF, VTI, which covers most US stocks, and BND, which gives you a good overview of the US bond market. Take your age, and that will be the percentage of your portfolio in BND. The rest will be held in VTI. Adjust as you get older.

And that's it. Expats in other tax havens such as the Cayman Islands, or the Channel Islands will want to hold their portfolios in primarily British

Taxes

investments as their main currency is in Sterling (unless you plan on retiring in a dollar denominated jurisdiction, then invest in American securities). Once again, **the rule of thumb is that you should invest according to the currency of the place where you plan to retire**. If you plan on retiring in the UK, but are working in the Gulf, you should invest mostly in the British market. If you are planning on retiring in the United States, you should invest in the American market. If you are planning on retiring in Europe, invest in European securities. If you plan on retiring to a developing economy, it doesn't matter where you invest so long as you invest in currencies which are strong and stable, i.e. developed economies.

What about expats living in tax havens that don't use the Euro, pound or dollar? I would suggest you invest in a **world stock index fund** for the stock portion of your portfolio, and then invest in the **US bond market**. US government backed bonds are the least likely to default of any bonds issued in the world, and the low price of credit default swaps against them reflects that. Most financial exchanges fall together as was shown in this most recent global recession, and investors around the world scrambled to buy US government bonds in an epic flight to quality. These bonds are seen by most investors as a **safe refuge** from stocks. They should be a part of any dollar heavy portfolio.

For nationalities other than Americans, living in a tax haven means never having to use retirement accounts, or bothering to hold bonds and stocks in separate accounts. Your returns will certainly be greater over time compared with someone living in a country that taxes capital gains. However, don't think this means you should take extra risk. In my experience living overseas in tax havens, I felt there was an unending supply of local businessmen trying to convince me to invest locally or invest in some exotic instrument I didn't understand. Ignore them. Stick to what you know, and that means stick with investing at home.

Some of you might say that you should take advantage of a local booming economy. You already are. Your job is an investment that you made in the local economy. You've already made a tremendous investment locally. Investing in developed economies is a way of diversifying your investments. Local financial exchanges in the Gulf and similar areas are opaque and have very small market capitalizations. That makes them volatile and risky. Investing back home allows you to take advantage of the markets with the best long term outlook and the strongest past performance (not that past performance is usually a good measure of future performance!).

You must remember: **there are taxes on investments by foreigners**. If you are not an American and decide to invest in American securities, you can expect to be taxed on your investment. If you are American and invest in European securities, again, you can expect to be taxed. Living in a tax haven means not facing local taxes, but you will always face the taxes of the countries you invest in.

Chapter Nine – Final Thoughts

Now do you know if and when you should leave your new country? You think you've found paradise. You have a beautiful home, the weather is perfect and the local cuisine is delectable. However you notice substantial **unrest** in the streets. From what you can gather from other expatriates and from reading your home country's newspapers on the internet (the local newspapers are highly censored), your new country's government is corrupt, incompetent, and has angered many citizens.

When to leave and come home

While living in Bahrain, I noticed civil unrest on an almost weekly basis. It usually came in the form of small demonstrations with burning tires blocking roads. It rarely became worse than that. Why didn't I leave? The

Bahrainis I knew reassured me that this activity was "normal". My fellow expats didn't seem to care either.

It all reminded me of that scene from the film *Godfather II*. Michael Corleone is in Cuba and discussing investing a substantial sum of money in the local economy. Earlier in the day he saw a Cuban rebel commit suicide with a hand grenade while being arrested. The resulting explosion killed a police captain. Michael is reassured that this is typical Cuban behavior. Later in the film, Fidel Castro comes to power.

There really is no clear solution. I suggest letting your nearest consulate or embassy know your location. I also suggest mapping out the quickest route from your home to the consulate in case of trouble.

I don't mean to sound paranoid. We live in an era of lessening unrest and growing wealth. However, corrupt poor countries have not learned to distribute that wealth as equitably as others leading to unrest and unhappiness. Understand the country you are moving to. Learn about its people.

Other expats can be both a great help and an obstacle

Guides for living abroad will portray your fellow expats as a source of information and assistance, and wonderful neighbors to boot. While all of that is certainly possible, and is usually the norm, not all expats are wonderful.

Expats are not necessarily like other people from back home. They leave their home country for a variety of reasons, not all of them good. Some don't fit in, others are running away from problems. That is not to say that

Final Thoughts

every expat you meet is a potential serial killer or fugitive. On the contrary, the restrictions placed against criminals from moving abroad make it highly unlikely you will meet a criminal on the lam. There is an issue however, with meeting what I call the typical **second chance expat.**

The second chance expat is someone who couldn't cut the mustard back home in his or her career, and views their new foreign home as a place where they can live cheaply, work semi-competently yet get paid well due to their status as a westerner abroad, and as a place where they can take advantage of the easy going nightlife and the companionship it might provide. The second chance expat literally views living abroad as a second chance at life.

This type of expat appears more often in countries that are **poorer** and that have a reputation for large **sex trades**. While this type of individual is certainly a down on his luck type (and they are typically male, though there is a female version), they are not all bad. The beauty of living abroad is that even those who lack the wherewithal to prosper back home can bring their skillset to another country and add to it in some way.

The other issue with living in expat communities is **gossip**. In my experience with the small number of Americans living in Dubai I felt they tended to be **clannish** and distrustful of outsiders. They also held themselves apart from other expats, even those of similar cultures like Canadians! Expat communities tend to cluster around a social club of some sort, as well as in certain neighborhoods.

There are tremendous benefits to associating with your country's expats. You will undoubtedly find people who know and understand your new country better than you. You may find contacts that can help you navigate government bureaucracies, and aid you if you run into trouble. One of my closest friends in the Persian Gulf was another American, and he was invaluable in assisting me in my occasional issues with local laws and customs. Without his help, I would have had a much rougher time. I met this person and his wife through an American business club in Dubai. The club introduced me to a few lifelong friends, and by avoiding the infighting and gossiping going on in the club, I was able to avoid many of the bad things associated with expat clubs.

In conclusion, look at expat clubs as a way to take a break from the local culture and to get a flavor of your home country. But don't get too involved in activities of the club, or you may get swept up in the infighting and politics that are commonplace in any club.

Visit first

Wherever you decide to move, if you take only one piece of advice away from this book, follow this one: **visit first**. And by visit I don't mean a week or two, I mean at least a month. Even more importantly, you should visit in different seasons in order to get a better picture of what you will have to deal with year round.

Here's a bit of strange advice: be sure to be in the country when a storm hits. In drier countries where rainfall is rare, the average person is unused to wet weather. Mudslides occur, people wreck more on the roads, no one has an umbrella. When I was growing up in Los Angeles, this was a yearly occurrence, and the roads became wet and dangerous. In dry climates oils trapped in asphalt will rise to the surface of the roads during rainstorms and make the roads even more slick and dangerous.

Final Thoughts

Have an escape plan

As I have discussed before, an expat should always keep open the option of leaving his home at a moment's notice. While stability in most countries occurs more often than turmoil, the poorer the country you live in, the more likely you will see:

- Street demonstrations, particularly against the government
- Intense poverty and unhappiness on the part of the poorest
- Rampant crime including burglary and murder
- Enormous inequities in wealth, with an upper class that cares little about its fellow citizens
- An incompetent government that does little for its people and rewards only the wealthiest of its citizens
- A despairing and lazy local population that is fed up and pessimistic about the future
- Infrastructure in need of repair

All these things are factors in turmoil and societal breakdown. However, none of them is enough to result in your needing to leave the country. So when is it apparent that a revolution is around the corner?

The tell tale sign of a revolution is the **massive street protest**. I'm not talking about five hundred college kids protesting in front of the university library, I mean **half a million** everyday people protesting vigorously in front of the main government offices, particularly the President/Prime Minister/Emperor's palace whatever that may be called.

Revolutions almost always occur when the average people from all around the country, even the countryside are protesting. When you see these people protesting, you know the end is near. Professional protesters such as students, hip urban young people, union professionals, these groups demonstrate regularly. But there are never enough of them to make a difference. The army which protects the leadership is made up of working class people and the rural poor. If the army is forced to fire on its own kind, it will lay down its arms and let the revolution commence. If the army is ordered to shoot students, young people, etc., it will happily do so. This is exactly what occurred in 2009 in **Iran** and is the key reason that revolution failed.

Some countries are culturally more inclined to protest and have street demonstrations such as **Argentina** and **France**. But these demonstrations almost always mean nothing. They never are representative of the whole of the country, and are done just to get a slightly larger handout or tax break from the government. So don't be worried. But if you see massive demonstrations in those countries lasting weeks, with the army facing off against them, then you should be panicking.

Evacuation

There may come a moment in your time abroad when you will have to leave because the country around you is falling apart, and your continued stay in the country might lead to your being killed. Frequently in times like this the best thing to do is to head to your nearest consulate or embassy. The embassy will have **well armed** security staff that are trained for such eventualities, including the evacuation of citizens and staff living in the country.

If things erupt into full rebellion, get to the embassy or consulate as fast as possible. They will figure out how to get you out. In all likelihood you will

Final Thoughts

be allowed to leave under **cease fire** conditions. The rebels won't want to create a diplomatic incident by shooting embassy staff.

What they will do is shoot people who are acting **suspiciously,** trying to ram through barriers, or trying to sneak out for whatever reason. If you do this, they will most likely think you are one of their former political leaders trying to **elude punishment** for various crimes, and they will try to kill you. Do not be this person. Go to the embassy and hope for the best.

There is however, the possibility of an **Iran** scenario. In 1978 and 1979, Iran overthrew the Shah and instituted a theocracy that is in power to this day. That group purposely took over the US embassy and held everyone there hostage for 444 days. No other embassies were taken over. In that case, the United States was seen by the new government as the protector and benefactor of the Shah.

Generally if you are a citizen of a western country and you make it into the embassy, you will be safe. However, in the case of the United States and to a lesser extent Britain and France, occasionally the local people will view these countries as allies of the old government that has just been overthrown. The US, Britain and France still maintain influence well beyond their borders, and are despised by many abroad for this reason. In countries where this influence is seen as non-existent, if you are a citizen of the US, Britain or France, you are probably safe. In other countries, particularly in the Middle East, not so much. Tread more carefully if you have one of these passports. Many parts of Latin America also view the United States with some hostility, and as having too great an influence in the region.

If a violent uprising is occurring and the local government is toppled, the rebels may be looking for foreigners to **hold hostage** in order to secure ransom and/or credibility. When rebels overthrow a government, the last act of that government is frequently to **loot the country.** That means taking foreign currency, namely US dollars and Euros, as well as whatever gold reserves there may be. The new government that comes to power has a severe dilemma. They must secure foreign currency and gold in order to pay debts and to make sure that their own currency is not **worthless,** as currencies usually become worthless when a government is overthrown. Foreign hostages are usually held for ransom and to get dollars from a foreign power, usually the United States.

Rest assured though: You are worth more alive than dead. You are worth money and political prestige as a passport holder of a western country. If the locals wanted you dead, you'd have no chance for escape. If you are captured, it's highly likely that you are being kept around for a reason.

Go for it

No amount of reading and preparation can truly prepare you for a career overseas. You simply have **bite the bullet** and get on the plane. Expats are a different lot. They may have an issue with the country they grew up in. They may find their home country unable to give them the job and career they were hoping for. They find the solution to their problems in moving overseas.

In the end this book seeks to be a very basic outline for a career abroad. It is drawn from my experience, and from the experience of the hundreds of expats I worked with and knew while living overseas. This book seeks to

Final Thoughts

give you the financial foundation necessary to achieve some measure of success. The rest is up to you.

For more information

For more information on the financial aspects of being an expat and for access to my daily thoughts, visit my blog at **www.expatinvesting.org**. You can email me any questions you have about this book or about being an expat through the site as well. I hope you've enjoyed reading this book as much as I've enjoyed writing it, and I hope it gives you the insight necessary to live and work successfully in whatever country you choose.

Index

401K, 148

Academic Ranking of World Universities, 93

accumulation phase, 141

Afghanistan, 10, 83, 129, 139

age, 19, 21, 90, 121, 144, 146, 153, 192, 224

Age, 90

Agence France Presse, 99

aid, 88, 229

air conditioning, 42, 180

Akrotiri and Dhekelia, 61

Albert Einstein, 151

alcohol, 179, 184, 195

alcoholism, 194, 195

Amnesty International, 94, 95

Andorra, 189, 208, 218

Anguilla, 62, 218

Antigua and Barbuda, 54, 62

apartment, 30, 34, 35, 40, 41, 42, 44, 46, 192, 222

Arabic, 70, 160

Argentina, 50, 61, 138, 139, 192, 209, 214, 232

Aruba, 62

Asda, 102, 179

Asia, 37, 70, 77, 91, 92, 172, 189, 191, 214

Associated Press, 99, 100

Astra, 167

ATM, 173, 174

attorney, 119

austerity, 51, 58

Australia, 16, 55, 57, 59, 89, 138, 153, 172, 182, 189, 191, 197, 208, 211, 215

Australian dollar, 55, 57

Canada, 16, 55, 57, 59, 89, 127, 137, 138, 153, 182, 188, 211

Cape Verde, 63

career, 3, 5, 9, 10, 11, 13, 21, 23, 24, 33, 65, 66, 67, 68, 74, 75, 76, 87, 92, 93, 95, 98, 103, 104, 106, 117, 119, 135, 141, 148, 151, 152, 176, 229, 234

Caribbean, 44, 64, 171, 213, 214

Carre-four, 179

cash, 13, 66, 176, 177, 178

Catholic Church, 97

Cayman Islands, 17, 62, 64, 218, 224

Central African Republic, 63

Central America, 185, 186, 214

Central Bank, 55, 56, 58, 101

CEO, 67

Chad, 63

Chevrolet, 166

Chile, 214

China, 62, 89, 91, 92, 139, 164, 178, 179, 185, 210

Citibank, 173

citizenship, 124, 128, 129, 130, 131, 132, 135, 136, 137, 139, 219

Ciudad Juarez, 39, 185

civil partnerships, 188

clothes, 196, 198, 199

Colombia, 185, 210

Colorado, 58

common law marriages, 188, 189

Comoros, 63

compound interest, 151, 152

corruption, 18, 31, 35, 43, 169, 181, 182, 183, 184, 200, 227, 228

Corruption Perception Index, 181

cost of living, 208

Costa Rica, 192, 210, 214

Cote d'Ivoire, 63

cover letter, 105, 106, 108

credit card, 152, 156, 177

credit default swaps (CDS), 49, 50, 51, 225

crime, 12, 18, 128, 131, 132, 185, 187, 193, 194, 199, 231

Croatia, 189

Cuba, 62, 228

Curacao, 63

currencies, 5, 39, 49, 50, 51, 52, 53, 54, 55, 56, 57, 58, 59, 60, 61, 62, 63, 64, 65, 66, 68, 69, 155, 175, 224, 225, 234

currency, 39

CV, 76, 100, 101, 104, 105, 108

Cyprus, 210

Czech Republic, 189, 210

debit card, 177

default, 49, 50, 52, 55, 57, 58, 59, 60, 61, 66, 148, 225

Denmark, 59, 63, 138, 181, 189, 191, 210

devaluation, 51, 54, 59, 60, 66

developed, 42, 44, 205, 206

developed country, 12, 18, 20, 42, 56, 65, 66, 69, 72, 74, 78, 88, 134, 137, 147, 175, 183, 205, 206

developing country, 19, 24, 42, 59, 60, 61, 65, 66, 88, 126, 134, 163, 173, 198

development, 34, 68, 88, 96, 191

disabled access, 192

Djibouti, 62

dollar, 34, 39, 50, 52, 54, 55, 56, 57, 60, 61, 62, 64, 65, 68, 80, 92, 97, 114, 118, 122, 152, 155, 156, 161, 167, 171, 175, 199, 204, 224, 225, 234

domicile, 134, 221, 222, 223

Dominica, 62

Dominican Republic, 213

Dow Jones Industrial Average
(DJIA), 145

driving, 45, 47, 159, 161, 162,
163, 164, 165, 166

drugs, 20, 39, 185, 186

dual citizenship, 124, 131, 132,
137

Dubai, 10, 29, 30, 69, 72, 79, 82,
83, 90, 101, 102, 106, 112,
133, 134, 167, 170, 178, 184,
222, 229, 230, 254

early retirement, 149

earthquake, 44

East Asia, 214

East Caribbean Dollar, 62

East Timor, 62

economic growth, 22, 29, 165,
169

Ecuador, 62, 189

education, 21, 91, 92, 93, 95, 99,
105, 120, 126, 190

Egypt, 198, 210

El Salvador, 62

electronic stability control, 162

English, 42, 43, 70, 90, 91, 92,
93, 96, 100, 101, 102, 106,
160, 161, 179

Equatorial Guinea, 63

Eritrea, 62

escape plan, 231

estate taxes, 220

Ethiopia, 70, 210

Euro, 47, 54, 55, 56, 57, 58, 60,
61, 62, 63, 64, 65, 68, 148,
156, 224, 225, 234

Europe, 10, 16, 28, 37, 39, 50,
51, 52, 53, 55, 56, 57, 58, 67,
91, 92, 94, 99, 104, 127, 137,
147, 148, 150, 172, 175, 179,
184, 189, 191, 192, 197, 199,
206, 208, 215, 219, 225, 226

European Union, 50, 51, 55, 56, 57, 58, 91, 104, 148, 169, 219

Euro-zone, 56, 58, 61

evacuation insurance, 206, 207

exchange traded fund (ETF), 154, 155, 224

expat, 10, 11, 12, 13, 15, 16, 18, 19, 20, 21, 22, 23, 25, 27, 29, 32, 33, 35, 37, 39, 42, 43, 45, 46, 47, 50, 52, 56, 60, 65, 67, 68, 69, 70, 71, 72, 73, 74, 75, 76, 77, 78, 79, 82, 84, 85, 86, 88, 89, 90, 94, 96, 99, 105, 112, 113, 115, 116, 117, 119, 127, 128, 129, 130, 131, 133, 134, 135, 141, 143, 157, 161, 169, 170, 183, 184, 185, 186, 187, 188, 190, 192, 193, 194, 195, 196, 206, 209, 211, 213, 217, 218, 219, 225, 227, 228, 229, 230, 231, 234, 235

Expat Investing, 3, 13, 235, 254

Fascism, 58

Federal Reserve, 55, 58

Fidel Castro, 228

finance, 18, 55, 101, 254

financial planning, 22

financial sector, 53, 59, 176

finding work, 79

Finland, 138, 182, 191

Florida, 46

Ford Foundation, 97

foreign debt, 57, 59

foreign exchange market, 55

foreign office, 74, 76, 78

foreigner, 39, 40

France, 17, 56, 105, 133, 138, 153, 189, 206, 207, 221, 222, 232, 233

franchise, 74, 75, 76, 78

French Polynesia, 63

frugality, 150

FTSE, 147

About the Author

Rick Todd is the author of this book and forthcoming books related to finance, travel and overseas living. He is an American who lived abroad for four years in three different countries, including the United Kingdom, the United Arab Emirates (specifically the Emirate of Dubai), and the Kingdom of Bahrain. He is a graduate of Loyola Law School in Los Angeles, and Boston University. He specializes in writing and communications on financial services topics and currently works in the area of public relations. He is an avid traveler and has traveled to more than twenty different nations (and counting). He writes a blog at the site **Expat Investing** which can be found at www.expatinvesting.org.